GROWING FROM THE ASHES

LEARNING FROM THE MURDER OF MY DAUGHTER ABOUT LIFE AFTER EARTH

SHEILA LOWE

Write
Choice
Ink
ESTABLISHED 2021

ISBN-10-978-1-970181-43-2 (Paperback)
ISBN-13-978-1-970181-42-5 (EPUB)
ASIN-(EPUB) B0BZX2DX7G

This book is a work of fiction. Names, characters, businesses, organizations, places, events, incidents are the product of the author's imagination or are used fictitiously. Any resemblance to actual events, locals, or persons, living or dead, is coincidental.

Cover Design, Illustrations: Scott Montgomery

Printed in the United States of America
PUBLISHING HISTORY
Write Choice Ink, Print and Digital Copy, April 4, 2023

www.sheilalowebooks.com
www.sheilalowe.com

Dedication

*To my children, Jennifer, Erik and Benjamin, who
in their own inimitable ways have made my life
on earth worth the trip.*

*And, to my friend Bob Joseph, without whom I would not
have written any book. Thank you for the important role
you have played in my story*

For Jennifer

She was a woman of fiery power
Who chose her own path.
Hers, no one else's.
Her strength eclipsed a thousand trials
Under pressure that molds diamonds.
The curves in the road were always
    hairpin turns for her,
The dips, always deep potholes.
Never a molehill,
Always Everest.
Still, she pressed on.
She cried and raged and burned,
She bent in two but never broke.
No wispy pinks or baby blues for her.
Queenly purple, sizzling red, Stygian black.
She was a woman of exotic beauty
Who never knew how beautiful she was
She was a woman well loved,
Who never knew how well loved she was

Contents

Chapter 1

February 19, 2000, 11:30 a.m.

W hen you pick up the ringing phone, you don't expect that a careless verbal match is about to be lit and set your world ablaze.

It's Saturday morning and I'm dashing around the house, a whirlwind of activity, preparing for a forensics conference in Reno. I have to figure out what I need to pack for the three-day trip, make arrangements for a ride from the airport to the hotel. Talk to the friend I'll be rooming with. Make sure my husband and adult son have enough food while I'm away—not because they are helpless, but because we take care of each other that way. Oh, and the cats. Must remember the cat food for Fritz and Sugar.

In the midst of all the crazy, my cell phone rings; a number I don't recognize. This is 2000, and only close friends and family have that number. Thinking that it's probably a misdial, I follow the ring tone and dig the phone out from under a stack of papers on my desk. I answer, hiding my impatience. "Hello?"

The voice I hear is male, unfamiliar, and expressionless. "—is Kenneth Lowe there?"

In my surprise at his request, I miss who he says he is. "Why are you calling my ex-husband on my cell phone?" I ask, confused. "We've been divorced twenty years."

Instead of answering, he moves right to his next question. "Do you know Jennifer Lowe?"

My stomach tightens. Two months ago, my daughter was placed in a mental health facility on a 5150 hold. That's the legal term for the involuntary commitment of an adult who is in a mental health crisis. Jen had freaked over some boudoir photos she'd had taken by a friend of a friend. Afraid that he would post them online when he refused to give her the negatives, she'd had a meltdown. Things went from bad to worse and her boyfriend, Tom Schnaible, called 911.

Tom carried the credibility and weight of working as a special agent for the federal government, so the doctors listened when he said Jen was suicidal and should be locked up.

She phoned from the hospital. "It's not true," she swore. "Tom is the crazy one, not me. Get me out of here. Please!"

Jen was twenty-seven, which left me powerless to do more than listen to her anguish and fury at being locked up, and to tell her that I loved her.

After the initial 72-hour evaluation period, the doctors refused to release her unless she would 'admit' that she wanted to kill herself. After a week-long standoff, they gave up and let her go.

Now, a stranger is calling me about her. What has she got herself into this time?

With an inward sigh, I mentally check off a few possibilities: jailed for shoplifting? It's been ten years since the last time. Picked a fight at a party in Mexico? A car accident with her friend, the Hell's Angel?

Has she harmed herself after all? *Please, God, not that.*

The questions tumble around in my head and my heart is racing as I say, with the dread of past experience, "She's my daughter. What about her?"

Holding my breath, I brace for bad news. But whatever I am expecting to hear, there is nothing that can prepare me for what this stranger has to say. He says it baldly, and without preamble or warning. The caller is Investigator Joe Homs of the Orange County California Sheriff's Department. He is the one who ignites the match and drops the bomb that changes my life forever: "I'm sorry to tell you, your daughter has been murdered."

Chapter 2

It can't be true

People who have experienced major trauma say things like, "my life flashed before my eyes." For me, time has stopped. I cannot process what I just heard; it's not making sense. I hold the phone away from me and stare at it as if it's a rattlesnake that suddenly reared up off my desk and bit me in the face.

It can't be true. It has to be a sick joke. You don't give this kind of news over the phone. There's a sheriff's station only two miles away. Surely, if it was true they would come to our door. I'd told Homs that I was on my cell phone. There can be no good way to deliver this kind of news, but what if I'd been driving on the freeway? All this is spinning through my head as I gasp out, "Hold on. Wait. Hold on. You have to tell my husband."

I yell for Bill, who is in our bedroom drinking one of many beers, and push the phone at him, shaking my head, unable to speak coherently. My older son, Erik, who lives with us, appears in the hallway, wanting to know what has happened. He must have recognized the panic in my voice.

"Was it Tom?" I hear myself asking urgently, while Bill is still on the phone, still listening to the investigator. *Was it Tom?* My gut tells me the answer even before he ends the call and turns to me with tears in his eyes. He nods. "He killed himself, too."

Right away, I start calling people. It's what I do and I hate that about myself. It's as if I'm trying to make that old saying come true: trouble shared is trouble halved. Some kinds of trouble cannot be diminished, no matter how many times it is shared.

I have no clue how I am going to tell Ben, my youngest, that he no longer has a sister. Despite the five-year gap between them, they are as close as twins. Maybe it's because they are both Sagittarians they 'get' each other in ways others don't. Though Jen always told people she was a Scorpio. She liked the intensity and power that she believed Scorpios possessed, and she was actually born on the cusp...

Oh my God.

We have to call Ken, her father. Bill takes on that appalling task. And Ken's brother, Jen's uncle Doug—they were close. And Rick, my brother, my best friend; our sister, Sara.

Minutes later, Rick and I are sobbing together over the phone, and even though I understand how it happened—maybe even why—still, none of it makes any sense.

In the end, it falls to Erik to break the news Ben, to his younger brother.

How? How? How?

I should call my mother, and I will. But that's another story. My close friends—what can they say? We are all in shock.

Late in the afternoon, a reporter from the *L.A. Times* calls, deceptively kind, to ask questions. The *Orange County Register*, too. Against my better judgment, I talk to them.

In my long career as a forensic document examiner and handwriting analyst, and as a mystery writer, too, I've been interviewed on TV, radio, blogs, podcasts, magazines, newspapers—I've done them all—and the one thing I've learned for sure: the news media inevitably get it wrong. They put quotation marks around stuff they've made up out of whole cloth; they skew the story the way they want it to sound. I don't want that to happen this time, so I make sure I am very clear.

I should have known better. The newspaper headline blares:

"INS Agent Kills Live-in Girlfriend"

In a mood to split hairs, I call the reporter and demand a correction. It was *her* apartment, not his. Tom Schnaible was the live-in, not Jen.

Like it matters. They're both dead.

Chapter 3

Red flags

A mere nine months earlier, Jennifer's friend, Preston, had introduced her to his brother, Tom. They fell for each other in the way soulmates do—as if they had been together over many lifetimes—as if there could be no other partner in the world. One problem: Tom was married, with a nine-year-old daughter, Elizabeth, whom he adored.

Perhaps ironically, Jen, separated from her husband, Scott Albertson, refused to be the Other Woman. Tom surprised her by immediately filing for divorce and insisting on moving into her upstairs apartment in a complex in Lake Forest, twenty-five miles south of Disneyland. He was understandably heartbroken when his wife promptly took their child and moved to Boston. His wife was probably heartbroken, too.

Tom learned that I was a professional handwriting analyst and wanted me to tell him what his handwriting said about him.

Over the years, my work in behavioral analysis has offered some remarkable insights into behavior and mental state, whether in the hiring process, or for individuals who wanted to know themselves better. And, naturally, when your mom is a handwriting analyst, you bring home samples of the people you are dating. I've issued many comments on my kids' friends and partners based on their handwriting, so when Tom wanted to send me a sample of his, I was as eager to see it as he was to hear my analysis.

Handwriting cannot reveal *everything* about the writer, but it can be very telling. Unfolding the letter Tom sent me, my heart sank as if it were chained to a 10-ton anchor.

The red flags that jumped off the page might as well have been a fire alarm blaring *Danger! Danger! Danger!* The note I scribbled on a Post-it: "potential for explosive behavior" is still stuck to the original sample.

Jennifer had already survived a couple of relationships that kept me up nights. She went for the dangerous ones, like Emery, who tattooed his name on her shoulder and pushed her into shoplifting and returning the goods for cash. That cost her a week in jail and a lifetime ban from Nordstrom department stores.

When she was released in the middle of the night, it was one of the few good ones—Patrick Palomino, a kind and supportive guy she had dated briefly—who went with me to pick her up from Sybil Brand Institute (a nice-sounding name for the women's jail). The good guys never lasted long with her. She was drawn to the ones who would hurt her.

During that week of incarceration, Jen witnessed sights that scarred her. Watching helplessly as a young woman having a seizure died because the jailers refused to allow anyone to give her aid. Inedible food. Horrendous jailhouse conditions. And yet, the trauma of that experience failed to stop her from diving into a relationship with a convicted felon. Being a felon doesn't make him a bad guy. Nick isn't the one who killed her. He even went with her to try and retrieve those boudoir photos that put her in the psych hospital. Something in that girl made people want to help her.

Things got physical with Nick, though who was at fault is in question. When neighbors called 911 during a loud fight one night, the female police officer who showed up said there was a scratch on his back, but nothing to indicate that he had struck Jen. She was arrested and jailed once again.

In another altercation with Nick, Jen suffered a sprained wrist and possible detached retina (no, he wasn't arrested). Following her release from the hospital she drove the 100 miles north to our house, looking for a safe place. Early the next morning, she was on the phone, begging him to take her back.

After her death, Nick told me about a time when she was trying to goad him into an argument (she was really good at pushing all the right buttons).

He didn't want to fight and risk arrest, so he walked himself to the nearby police station with her yelling at him the whole way.

§

What alarmed me most about Tom's handwriting were the clear signs of an authoritarian personality. According to the American Psychological Association, the personality traits of the authoritarian personality type include great deference to authority figures while demanding subservience from those they regard as lower status; highly simplified conventional values (black/white, no grey), and hostility toward people who deviate from conventional mores. Plus, they have a strong need for control.

It's not unusual to find those traits in law enforcement officers, which Tom was. For my daughter, though, there could not be a worse type. To say parenting Jen was a struggle is like saying wrestling a hungry tiger is a little tricky. I'd been a single mother since she was eight and I was far from strict, but she resisted any measure of control I ever exerted.

Not long before she was killed Jen told me, "I've known what I needed since I was six years old. You should have let me make my own decisions."

That made me laugh. "It was my job to parent," I told her, though my words fell on deaf ears. "Not to let you do whatever you wanted."

Studies have shown that the authoritarian personality type develops in people who had highly critical and harsh parents. Tom said that his father had been abusive, and then absent from his life. Some researchers believe that because the person was not given a chance to express negative feelings toward their parents for being so strict and critical, they take their hostility out on others whom they perceive as weaker than themselves. As I was finding out, hostility like that can lead to terrible consequences.

To add to the list of negatives, Tom's handwriting revealed a tendency for unstable and potentially violent behavior. As I'm not a doctor, I cannot diagnose illness. However, certain distinctive features in handwriting may point to areas of the body where there are physical problems. For example, assuming it's not an artifact of a bad pen, a tiny dot of ink in the writing line may point to a circulatory problem. The area of handwriting where the feature appears indicates where in the body the issue may be. A dot at the top of an 'o' or 'e,' for instance, may indicate a problem in the abdominal area, perhaps the stomach. In Tom's case there were dents at the tops of upper loops, and tiny light spots in the ink.

"Did you ever have a head injury?" I asked him.

"How did you know that?" he asked, shocked. "I was hit in the head so hard I was almost blinded."

Law enforcement is a dangerous occupation, and he said it had happened on the job. I doubt that Tom, a former Marine, ever walked away from a fight or a challenge to his authority. After the murder/suicide, his brother fought to have him buried in Arlington National Cemetery, citing good works he had done. The request was rejected. One evil act wipes away a thousand good ones.

Tom told me he was in treatment for severe headaches. Add to that alcohol abuse—they both regularly drank too much—the police reports quoted neighbors describing him as "falling down drunk." Jen had been working on getting sober and called in tears when he mocked her for trying to quit drinking.

From what I could see, this was an explosion waiting to happen.

I tried to be tactful. "Tom, your handwriting shows a strong need to be in control, but if you try to control Jennifer, it's going to lead to big problems. You can't control her; she's always been extremely independent."

That was code for: she never listened to anyone (especially me), and her 'independence' had caused a fair amount of trouble. Until now, I'd held a secret belief that if she could just make it to twenty-two or twenty-three, she would grow up enough to be okay. I was off by four or five years.

The three of us, Jen, Tom, and I, talked at great length about what they would need to do to make the relationship work. I knew in my gut that my warnings would be ignored. I gave them anyway.

When he moved in with her and started calling me with complaints, and she called me with complaints, I reminded them of that conversation about his handwriting. A warning only works when the recipient heeds it.

Chapter 4

I can't sleep

It's two o'clock in the morning, fifteen hours after the news of our loss, and I am imagining what must have gone through her mind as Tom chased her down with that murderous piece of black metal he was so proud of. Had she felt the searing heat of the bullets as they ripped into her brain, her heart, her lungs? Grazed her cheek?

Can it be true? Is she really dead? Maybe she's in the coroner's refrigerator drawer, frantically fighting to get out. The coroner made a huge mistake on the death certificate. She is nowhere near 5'8, 150 pounds, as they have stated on the form.

Insult to injury.

I call and ask if they are sure they have the right body. They make the correction without apology.

When they met, Jennifer was twenty-six and petite at five-four, with the kind of exotic beauty that comes with being mixed race. Tom was thirty-four, six-four and weighed 235; a good-looking dude who worked as a special agent for what was then called the INS (Immigration and Naturalization Service). These days, it's known as Homeland Security. She was attracted to his physical strength and believed he would protect her.

Early in the relationship they came to visit and we liked him. They seemed happy. My daughter, whose sense of humor was as different from mine as chalk from cheese, telling us how Tom would scare the crap out of other drivers, brandishing his service weapon in pretend road rage. She thought it hilarious.

As part of his job, Tom taught hand-to-hand combat. Perhaps he hoped to impress Bill by showing him the high-power 40 caliber Beretta semi-automatic handgun he carried at all times. "I really like it," he told my husband. "It has good stopping power."

If we had known he would use it to stop my daughter with six bullets—one for every vital organ—could we have prevented this tragedy?

These are the thoughts running through my brain like a hamster on a wheel in the middle of the night and on into Sunday morning, alternating with memories of my last conversation with Jennifer, seven hours before she was killed.

$$\text{\Large ❧}$$

It's Friday evening before the murder/suicide. Bill and I are at Mulligan's, our favorite local restaurant. As I often do, I order their chicken breast with mushrooms and artichokes in a lemon butter sauce with pasta. Prime rib for Bill.

Mid-meal, Jennifer calls and wants me to email something to one of her professors at Saddleback College. She's pre-med. I don't know why she can't do it herself, but I agree that I will do it when I get home.

Then she starts complaining about Tom.

After the December incident with her freaking out about the boudoir photos, and being committed to the psych hospital, Tom's supervisor at the INS had given him an ultimatum: break up with her or lose his job. He had promised that he would, but when it came down to it, he did not break up with her, nor did he move out. What he did do, hoping to save his job, was ask Jen to recant the accusations she had recently made—that he had held her at gunpoint and threatened to kill her and himself.

On the morning of the murder-suicide they went to his supervisor and she capitulated.

In that last phone call, she assures me that after the nine month mistake she had made, getting involved with Tom, she is ready to leave the relationship. She and Scott are going to get back together and start a family. Never mind the part where she had left Scott, saying he was "too weak" when he pleaded with her to stay with him.

"Can I come and stay with you for a few days while I work it out?" she asks me.

I'm filled with relief that she is ready to take this big step. "Of course you can," I say giving Bill an apologetic glance across the table. Then, I add, "Hey, kiddo, we're out to dinner right now; can we talk about it tomorrow?"

"Sure," my daughter says, sounding cheerful and optimistic. "Talk to you then."

But there is no tomorrow.

Chapter 5

Small blessings

I am so grateful for the rare times we were able to do things together. With a distance of 100 miles between us, we didn't have a lot of chances to socialize.

When the kids were growing up, I never had much money left after paying the bills, but now, with them all grown, and I was married to Bill and successful in my handwriting analysis practice, pinching pennies wasn't a concern. So, driving down to Lake Forest and taking my daughter out to a nice restaurant and browsing at the Mall afterwards was a big treat for both of us. We'd shop at the cosmetics counter at Penney's or for clothes at TJ Maxx or Nordstrom Rack. These days, when I'm walking around those stores, I can't see her walking next to me, but I sometimes sense her presence. I ask Jen to help me find what I'm looking for.

January 30, 2000 was Superbowl Sunday, twenty days before she was killed. Bill was an avid football (or any sport, even golf) fan. Tom watched the game with him, while Jennifer and I went to the local Albertson's to pick up groceries for dinner.

She was always short of money, and we both knew I was going to buy whatever she asked for that day. Among a few other items, she picked out a special poppy seed salad dressing—a great choice—and a box of Lipton's tea. There are not a lot of memories I cherish with her, but that is one of them. I know it's ridiculous, but that box of tea has been in my pantry ever since, mostly unused.

The week after the Superbowl, Bill and I hosted a baby shower for the kids' cousin Lauren at Shanghai Red's in Marina del Rey. Jen was a little under the weather with a cold, but she was in her element when the whole family was together like that.

It was Jen who, after the years of being Jehovah's Witnesses and not celebrating holidays, pushed for Christmas and Thanksgiving as a family. She usually brought a friend or two—Marine friends of Scott's who didn't have their own family nearby. A photo that still makes me smile is of Jen and Erik preparing a turkey together at Bill's and my home in Valencia. Like most brothers and sisters, they didn't get along until they were older.

Since she's been gone, those events have fallen apart. They needed her energy behind them.

Chapter 6

Strange things happen

My first day as a daughterless mother. I'm thanking neighbors I've never spoken to who saw it on the news. They've brought condolences to our door, and casseroles I won't eat. Can't even think about eating.

I've reached the "at leasts," where you try to rationalize the inconceivable.

At least we knew who killed her; it wasn't some random stranger.
At least she wasn't kidnapped and tortured and left in an anonymous grave so we never knew what happened to her.
At least Tom killed himself, too.
At least I got to talk to her that last night.
At least it was quick.

Like that.

Over the next few days, weeks, months, things happen that cannot be explained in human terms.

I'm in my home office. It's the day after the murder. The phone rings. After the blow dealt by Joe Homs twenty-four hours ago, I am afraid to pick it up, dreading who might be on the line and what they might say.

"Hello?" I answer. "Hello," All I hear is a weird, loud staticky noise. "Who is this? Hello?"

I can hear a voice speaking as if from a very long distance. It's impossible to make out the words. And then, it's gone. Moments later, the same thing happens on my cell phone.

The fundamentalist religion I was raised in teaches that any contact with the spirit world is 'of the devil.' Thanks to my precious daughter I happily reject that belief. Jennifer is trying to reach me; I absolutely know it.

If only I knew what she was saying. Is she calling for help? Letting me know she has arrived safely on the Other Side? *Please let it be the latter.* I can't bear to think of her wandering around some nether world, not knowing what to do or where to go.

I'm grateful she wanted to reach out to me.

Later, I'm sitting at the dining table and I see her walk past the kitchen doorway. Just a glimpse, gone in an instant, but as real and present as you or me. Nobody believes me. They pretend to, but I can see they think I've lost it.

That same day I'm in the living room and catch a whiff of her perfume, *Tresor.* It's what she wanted for Christmas two months ago. I gave it to her along with a photo album I made her of her life. For the first time I can remember, she spontaneously hugged me and said the album was the best present I could have ever given her. She gave me a gift, too: a teapot and two mugs in a basket. The funny, pugnacious gingerbread man Christmas card signed, simply, "Jennifer," was so her. It's the only card she ever gave me.

My brother, Rick, has arrived for the funeral. We're in the living room when the stereo surprises us by turning itself on and playing *Storm at Sunup* by Gino Vanelli. Rick used to travel with a group of friends wherever Gino was playing. My brother and my daughter had become close over the last year. I think the music was her way of reaching out to him.

A few weeks so earlier, Jen and Tom had driven up to Valencia and the four of us climbed into Bill's car and headed for the Regal, or whatever the theater was in those days. She wanted me to see the new movie, *The Sixth*

Sense, and kept sneaking peeks at my reactions. She wanted me to love the movie as much as she did.

I did.

Around the same time, I read Richard Matheson's book, *What Dreams May Come.* Jen and I were both excited when the 1998 movie starring Robin Williams came out on TV, and we watched it together.

Both films are about life after death. Was it prescient that Jen was so fascinated by the topic? She had always believed she would die young.

Chapter 7

Eternal Valley

Monday

Bill and I are at Eternal Valley Memorial Park to make final arrangements. Which sounds so...final.

When we moved from Los Angeles to Valencia in 1993, seeing the cemetery on the hillside that flanked the 14 freeway I'd remarked that someday, I would like to be buried there.

Me. Not my only daughter.

Wearing a kindly salesman face, the funeral director takes us to a big showroom. Bill is listening to his spiel, but I zone out, only half paying attention to the costs of the casket, the rose spray to go on top, his fee, the minister's fee, the chapel rental, the burial plot. It probably should not surprise me to learn that even a not-fancy funeral adds up to $14,000. I am not about to stint on this occasion, but Bill, as always, generous and willing to spare no expense, insists on plunking down his credit card. The Victims of Violent Crime fund will pay part of it. And therapy, if we want.

I would rather have spent the money on her wedding to Scott. Before Tom entered the picture Jennifer and Scott had quietly gotten married in Las Vegas without telling anyone, planning to have a 'real' wedding with the dress and veil and reception later, when they could afford it. As John Lennon astutely pointed out, "Life is what happens when we're busy making other plans."

Her body will be transported from the coroner in Orange County on Wednesday, says the funeral director when we return to his office. I tell him that I want to see her straight away and he gently explains that she won't be 'ready for viewing' until Thursday, the day before the funeral. "But I'm her mother," I protest. "I've seen her at her worst."

Since then, I've read the autopsy report about the blood and the six bullet holes.

Chapter 8
Closing down a life

Tuesday

Bill, home from work on bereavement leave, is drinking a lot. That's nothing new, but it is the source of many bad feelings on my part. I had hoped that under the circumstances he might back off the beer for a while. Fat chance.

Something I say pisses him off. I never know what it's going to take, and it doesn't have to be anything of significance; an off-hand remark will do. When my husband is angry, he punishes me by refusing to talk. At all. Usually for a week. Then he will suddenly start yelling about whatever set him off, and once he's finished, it's all over and done. Typically, we go out to dinner and forget about it. Once, though, after a stupid misunderstanding, he didn't speak to me for three months. That was just before the second divorce.

Now, when I could use his support, he turns away from me in vengeful silence. My response to the dead air is to go about my business, do my own thing, and generally pretend he doesn't exist.

I get in the car and make the two-hour drive to Jennifer's apartment in Lake Forest.

It all feels a bit rushed—they aren't even buried yet—but I can't stand to leave the place as it was when Tom gunned down my baby girl. I certainly don't want to return here a second time, and the March rent on her apartment will be due in a few days. It's got to be cleared out and cleaned.

Ken, the father of my three kids, has arrived from Utah along with his nine-year-old daughter and second wife, Vivian, who used to be our babysitter. They are waiting at the apartment complex with some of Ken's siblings:

Douglas, Debby, Donna. I have known them for most of their lives, but they don't speak to me because, like my mother, they are Jehovah's Witnesses and I am shunned. Kind of like Bill, who is shunning me, but they have the excuse of religion.

I was officially disfellowshipped from the church for leaving my marriage to Ken. For JWs disfellowshipping means that "no one is to say a greeting" to you. Even close family members are expected to give the disfellowshipped person the cold-shoulder. The only exception being when there is 'family business' to discuss. You'd think the murder of a close family member would count.

Our younger son, Ben, 23, and his friend Jimmy, have rented a moving truck to take away the furniture and put it in storage. For some reason, Erik, 25, is absent. Both of my boys are consumed with grief and rage that they were unable to protect their big sister.

The truth is, Jennifer wouldn't have welcomed their interference if her brothers had known of the threat against her and stepped in. What's more, if they had known and taken matters into their own hands, an unimaginable situation would have been made a million times worse.

As tragic as it is for Tom's little daughter, who has been told that her daddy had an accident, I thank God over and over that he killed himself, too, and spared us the trauma of a trial.

Parking my car, I notice two unfamiliar men who I guess are Tom's father and brother—who are there to pick up his personal effects. They are standing off to the side, as if they don't know what to do. I don't know what to do, either, so I go over and hug them and we cry together.

I'm told Tom's mother in Florida has been hospitalized. I was out when she called my office number, and I couldn't reach her when I called back. I snailmail her a couple of photos I had taken of her son, and a copy of *Talking To Heaven,* a book on the Afterlife by James Van Praagh. I never heard from her again. I wish we could have connected and shared our grief. For your child to be murdered is unspeakable. For your child to be a murderer is something I cannot even fathom.

Ken and I and Tom's father enter the apartment, where there is little evidence of the struggle that took place three nights ago. The empty rooms are patiently waiting for their occupants to come home and live in them.

The local battered women's shelter is coming for their clothes and the food in the kitchen cupboards. I stuff Jen's things into plastic bags for the charity to pick up. A box full of ammo on the top shelf of the bedroom closet goes to the police department. Tom's dad gets his books on war.

There were three topics my daughter and I could talk about without getting into an argument: cooking, cats, and tarot cards. Jen's collection of cookbooks and her many decks of cards are going home with me. Her stuffed animals and other miscellaneous items will be stored in our garage.

I fold some of her favorite pajamas, a sweatshirt she liked; a pair of warm socks that I will wear to keep her close. The fluffy white plush cat will sit in a bag for twenty years until Ben has a child, Cleo Ayla. Jennifer will never meet her niece in Germany. Not in the physical, anyway, though it's quite clear that they communicate with each other.

As a mystery writer, I am familiar with what homicide detectives call the murder book. One is constructed for every case to hold copies of interviews with witnesses and others, diagrams, reports, etc. I build my own personal murder book in a five-inch 3-ring binder, filling it with autopsy reports, police reports, death certificate, letters, statements, etc. There is also a zippered bag from the funeral home, stuffed with countless condolence cards that I cannot go back and re-read. Neither can I throw them away.

A *Little Mermaid* plastic figure goes into a box, along with a collection of ceramic mermaid figurines, and a mermaid print by John William Waterhouse that will occupy my living room wall. The mermaid lamp whose flat circular glass shade has already cracked and been repaired twice; all go in the box. So many mermaids. I wish I knew what they meant to her. Maybe she related to the mythical creature who gave up her voice for love.

Anything that has Jennifer's handwriting on it goes into the box. I will keep her emails, too, but there is nothing more personal than the handwritten list she made—pros and cons of being in a relationship with Tom Schnaible.

In her closet are the veil and gown we bought for the big wedding she will never have. She'd looked utterly radiant at the bridal shop when she tried it on. I will bury her in it.

Before leaving the apartment complex, Ken and I stop downstairs to meet Corey Hightower, the neighbor whose 911 call was played on NBC's *Extra* show in a segment about the murder-suicide and the danger signs I saw in Tom's handwriting. No matter how many times I hear Corey's shaken voice on the recording, it pierces my heart.

"Hey, man, my neighbor just shot his girlfriend,"

We want to thank him for trying to help our daughter that night.

Around 2:30 a.m. Corey was watching TV in his living room when a bloodcurdling scream cut through the night. Then another, and the sound of Jennifer running down the exterior stairs and crying outside Corey's apartment door. He brought her into his apartment, and his wife, seeing strangulation marks on her neck, asked if she was okay.

"No," Jennifer said through her tears. "Tom's crazy; I called 911."

I later learn that after our phone conversation at Mulligans, Tom and Jennifer went to Cook's Corner, a biker bar in Trabuco Canyon. She sometimes worked there, taking tickets at the door. A woman Jen knew—a one-night stand of Tom's—showed up and made trouble.

A furious Jennifer is like watching David Banner morph into the Incredible Hulk. After a confrontation with the woman, she stormed out of the bar, took the car, and went home, leaving Tom to walk the five or six miles to the apartment. By the time he arrived, he had worked up a head of steam. The strangulation marks on Jen's neck were the evidence.

Corey wanted her to stay put until the police got there. 911—should be a couple of minutes, right? But as time passed and no one showed, Jen started to worry about her cats and insisted on going back upstairs to make sure Tom wasn't mistreating them.

Over the next half-hour things were quiet. Then Corey heard noises on the stairs again and went to look out of his front window. His upstairs neighbors were both at the bottom of the staircase. Tom, "looking deranged," was dangling something in his hand and called out in a mocking tone: "I've got the keys."

As Jennifer turned to run for Corey's apartment, Tom raised his weapon and started shooting. The first shot propelled her across the patio. He kept on shooting.

Using his skills as a trained law enforcement officer, he took her down with six bullets. A seventh went through the wall of Corey's apartment and lodged in the entertainment center; an eighth in the handlebar of his little girl's bicycle. There were other bullets. I don't know where they landed.

Having carried out what he'd been threatening for weeks, Tom Schnaible strode to the the carport, got in his car, and drove towards the complex exit. It was at this moment, *forty minutes* after Jennifer told her neighbor she had called 911, and after Corey had made several 911 calls himself, the police deigned to show up.

Two minutes too late to save her life.

Seeing the police cars, Tom exited his vehicle. Leaving the engine running, he returned to Corey's front door, where Jennifer's body lay, her lifeless eyes staring at nothing.

Tom knelt on the ground and kissed her, then put the gun in his mouth and fired once.

Corey Hightower and his family had to climb through the window, over the two bodies blocking their front door, in order to leave their apartment.

The Sheriff's department repeatedly lied to me about why it took forty minutes to respond to those 911 calls on a quiet night (I obtained the records of all calls for the weekend). Finally, I took a formal statement from Corey, who told me what actually happened.

"I'll never forget her eyes," he said.

"What do you mean?"

"She was gone instantly."

Small mercies.

Chapter 9

A rainy drive to Hemet

We leave Corey's apartment with storm clouds gathering overhead. It occurs to me to be grateful that by the time we spoke with him, the blood had been washed from his patio.

Locking Jennifer's door behind us, I say goodbye to Ken, and to Tom's people. Ben and Jimmy have taken the moving van to the storage facility. It's time for me to meet up with Joe Homs at the animal shelter where the police placed Jen's cats, Charlie and Victor. Her older two, Fritz and Sugar, live with Bill and me. My brother has agreed to re-home these two near him in Hemet. Rick's stepdaughter, also a Jenny, will take Victor. Charlie will go to Heidi, his ex-wife. Like me, Jennifer loved all cats. But Charlie was her baby.

I'm feeling nervous about meeting this man who dropped the bomb on me. My go-to habit when dealing with trauma is to work, or think about work. A defense, I suppose. Inspector Homs and I are walking through the grounds to the special room where they keep the cats whose owners have been a victim of violent crime. Awkwardly, I blurt, "I'm a mystery writer. Maybe I can ask you some questions sometime."

What the hell kind of thing is that to say three days after your daughter has been killed in a murder-suicide? Homs fails to respond. What a jerk I am. It sounds so callous. Shame hits me all over again as I type the words.

In the cardboard carrier they share, Victor and Charlie are remarkably quiet as we load them into the passenger side foot well of my old Chrysler Le Baron convertible. The boxes of cookbooks and cards and other stuff I'm taking home with me occupy the backseat, the wedding dress and veil draped across them.

By the time I enter the Riverside Freeway for the seventy-five-mile drive east to Rick's home in Hemet, the sky is as grey as my mood and it's drizzling enough to turn on the wipers. Suddenly, something happens that has never happened before and never happens again.

The dome light in my car goes on. All by itself.

Or not.

No wonder the cats are being so good. Jennifer is riding with us. That makes me feel a teeny bit better.

Chapter 10

The viewing

It's the day before the funeral. Bill has relented and is speaking to me again.

We return to Eternal Valley and are taken to a viewing room. In the casket we chose is a life-size doll. That's what she looks like to me, anyway. Bill is in tears and I am fighting not to pass out.

My daughter would hate the way they made her look. I remember the countless hours she spent straightening the long brown hair they've curled into ringlets. The makeup is garish, her cheeks too pink. I guess it takes a lot of pancake to cover a bullet-grazed cheek.

The casket will be closed for the funeral. Jennifer, a much more private person than I am—a strong trait in her father's family—would be mortified to be put on display for everyone to look at.

Late that night I attempt to get some work done. The previous week, when life was still relatively normal, my colleague, Sharon Tschirhart, asked me to handle her clients while she was out of town. She often subcontracted me that way, and the work was welcome, so of course, I said yes.

Now, sitting at my computer I stare at the stack of six handwriting samples that rolled in for analysis via fax that morning, wondering how I'm going to complete this task. Sharon's client is expecting the reports. There's no way for me to reach her and tell her I will be burying my daughter tomorrow morning.

I can't let Sharon down. Just pick up the first handwriting, I tell myself. You can do it.

My fingers rest on the keyboard but nothing happens. After writing more than ten thousand analyses over my career, everything I ever knew about handwriting has deserted me. My mind is blank. The words simply will not come.

At midnight, I finally admit to myself that I can't do it, and go to join my sleeping husband.

Chapter 11

The funeral

Friday

The black knit dress I've decided to wear buttons all the way up the front. Gaps between the buttons mean I need to wear a slip underneath. I don't have a black slip. I rush to the nearby Mervyn's department store and grab the first one I see, then rush back home and get ready for something you can never be ready to do.

For the third time, we make the short drive to Eternal Valley. People have already begun to arrive and are waiting around outside. Bill stops the car in front of the cemetery chapel to let me out. When I step out of the vehicle my legs unexpectedly give way. Erik catches me.

How did we notify all these people? My dear friend Bob Joseph is there. He's the one who taught me how to read tarot and gave Jennifer psychic readings. And Roland Sparks, my very first therapist; he changed my life.

Some of Jen's best friends are here. Coulette is MIA, but there is April with her new baby, and Nicki, who I haven't met before and who looks so much like Jen that for a moment I think it's her and none of this is real. Rick. My sister, Sara, who at that time I seldom see. My son-in-law, Scott Albertson, is there as well, looking shellshocked.

Nick and some of her other friends, I hear later, are upset that they didn't know when and where the funeral was. In 2000, Facebook and Instagram are in the distant future. It's not so easy to rapidly share news.

The chapel is full. Erik and his girlfriend are seated next to me, but somehow, Ben and his girlfriend are in the row behind us. This bothers me, but I can't think how to fix it.

Officiating is the minister from the church Jen and her uncle Doug have been attending together. To open the service, he reads the poem I wrote for Jennifer just this morning—the one at the front of this book. I don't know what else he says. Ken took him aside ahead of time to make sure he isn't going to upset the handful of JWs in the chapel and say something religiously objectionable.

At the end of the minister's remarks Ben removes his suit coat and hands it to the funeral director to place with his sister when she is put in the ground. Erik has added something of his own in the pocket.

Everyone but Ken and I make their way out of the chapel. He has yet to see his daughter in death.

Our relationship has long been acrimonious, but now, we set the past aside and walk together to the closed casket. Just imagine how any father might react to seeing his child in a box.

Bill and I, Erik and Ben, Ken's family, the other mourners, all walk behind the hearse, following it up the steep hill. At the area where the graveside service and burial will take place the driver stops and opens the rear door. The pallbearers—my sons and Doug, Scott and Ken's stepsons, Isaac and Ryan—begin sliding the casket out of the hearse when the sudden loud BEEP BEEP BEEP of a car alarm startles us all.

The sound is coming from Doug's rental car in the parking lot nowhere near us. He isn't holding the key and no one is near the car. I squeeze Bill's hand and tell him what I am sure of: "There she is, letting us know she's here with us."

In my later afterlife studies, I learn that it's quite common for someone who has crossed over to attend their own funeral.

Following the graveside service, people mill around on the grass. The casket is suspended over the pit into which it will descend once we depart. Reluctant to leave my girl alone but surrounded by the hundreds of graves of strangers, I remain seated. The funeral director sidles over and speaks *sotto voce*. "No one is going to leave until you do." So, I take a deep breath, push myself off the chair, and chat with the other mourners; invite them to our house for refreshments.

To my great surprise, my mother and her husband Jerry show up at the house. I try to hug her but she's stiff as a board—the cliché fits. They were the first ones out the door of the chapel, like Ken, uncomfortable with a religious service that didn't conform to their complicated Jehovah's Witness beliefs about life and death. Having made their appearance, they refuse any food or drink and quickly take their leave. It's a long ride home to Banning and my mother, who struggles with vertigo, doesn't do well in the car. It's a pretty good excuse.

After a month of regular phone calls to comfort me, she will let me know that it's time for us to "go back to normal." To my mother, 'normal' means not speaking to me because I was kicked out of the religion 15 years earlier, and the JW organization requires I be shunned.

And then, everyone is gone and it's just the immediate family crowding our small living room.

Utterly drained, I lie on the couch, unable to do anything that requires thought or action.

Knowing we were going to need something to cheer us up—as if that is remotely possible—we have hoarded a new Eddie Izzard video for the occasion. Bill slides *Dress to Kill* into the VHS player and the "Executive Transvestite," as the British comedian calls himself, launches into his show.

Should we feel guilty for appreciating Eddie's clever jokes? I think it's probably okay to be grateful for the laughs he gives us through our tears.

Chapter 12

Coulette

I invited Coulette, one of Jen's best friends from her teenage days, to share some memories of their time together.

Jennifer came into my life in the 9th grade at a time when friends are the center of a teenager's world. At some point, we began hanging out together exclusively and became best friends. I was going through a phase and started to really challenge my grandmother, who I lived with, on respect and discipline. With Jennifer, one plus one equaled six as we both contributed to each other's bad behavior. She was not a bad influence per se, but she was further along in her wild phase, so it was easier for me to be shepherded into that lifestyle since I had a friend to do it with.

We attended different schools, but were mostly together after the school day. We traveled all over Los Angeles, taking the bus or walking the mile on foot between each other's houses, hanging out at Venice Beach, going to house parties, or shopping. Jennifer was adventurous and explored interests far beyond her years. We traveled to white witch shops, designed a prayer alter in her closet, and chanted "Nam Myoho Renge Kyo" at Buddhist temples. She somehow always connected her life to folks exploring how to better themselves. She pursued spiritual growth, and I was happy to tag along.

I spent almost every weekend at Jennifer's house. I was the worst about borrowing her clothes and not returning them. When I describe that time of my life to my military contemporaries after almost 30 years of service, I ask them if they have seen "The Lord's of Dogtown" movie. Haha—we lived the ghetto-by-the-sea lifestyle, getting into mischief at all hours of the day. I cringe now at how badly we treated Sheila, being disrespectful, using her things *[note from Sheila—finally, I know where my favorite blue knit dress disappeared to!]*, not telling her where we were. Jennifer and I were so focused on doing the things we wanted that we did not think about the consequences of our actions and how they stressed the people who loved us.

I was told that Jennifer had been on Oprah Winfrey for a piece on Children without a Conscience. It didn't really impact what I thought about her, as teenagers don't deeply discuss those type of things. I don't think we ever talked about it; however, Jennifer was leading the charge on us getting into mischief. One time she showed up at my high school with a black eye. She matter-of-factly told me the story of how she got it. We were always together, but Jennifer was reserved with her feelings and never discussed them. She talked about traumatic memories in her childhood (dropping her dad off at Disneyland, not having much contact with him) like it was a matter-of-fact event.

When Jennifer got a red Nissan truck we traded in our walking shoes for her wheels. During this time, a mutual friend was killed while riding his motorcycle after drinking. When we found out, she hugged me, one of the rare times we did that. She was a dichotomy of personality traits: wild, un-attached, and impulsive, but so much fun. She loved cats, made homemade food, forgave me when I ruined her clothes, and always wanted to explore new experiences. She was definitely the unicorn to my donkey.

In 1991, Jennifer got involved with a group of friends who were using a theft ring to generate income to buy drugs. I had dropped out of high school by this point and was aimless in my future plans. I went with her to a house with one of these folks, then to the mall when Jennifer tried to return stolen items for cash. The store was tracking us and Jennifer was taken in back to be questioned, while they let me leave. I waited in the parking garage for her, thinking this was not the way my life was supposed to go. I stopped hanging out with Jennifer at this point and dropped back into school. I left California six months later after I graduated from high school and went to live in Maryland with my Aunt and Uncle. The whole trajectory of my life changed from that point and my contact with Jennifer became very infrequent because we were on different coasts.

We spoke a handful of times; I knew she had married, was exploring being a nurse, etc. but our lives were moving in different directions. Years later when I was pregnant with my first child, a lifetime from my juvenile delinquent past, Sheila contacted me with the shocking news that Jennifer had been murdered. I remember immediately being sad that we had not had much contact in recent years, and I grieved for my future self who would not have the opportunity to share my grown-up years with Jennifer.

I have not had a best friend again and often think how my life could have been different if she was still in it—how we might have transformed as adults and laughed about our reckless teenage years from the vantage point of life experience.

Chapter 13

April

A note from Jen's adult best friend, April

At the funeral I asked if I could take one red rose because it reminded me of the beautiful red lipstick that Jen would wear when we went out. I promised her I'd be back and light her a black candle and have some drinks with her. I remember going to Sheila's house afterwards, but I was still so shocked, I don't remember much about that day.

I do remember thinking that she said she loves her cats so much that she would die for them. I would tell her to stop saying that and she would always respond, "Well, I would."

I couldn't believe that Tom, that PoS, was in my house; that I shook her killer's hand and sat down and had a beer with him. It makes me sick to this day that I met and invited a murderer into my house!

The memories I have of Jen are the crazy good times in all her different cars, our Disneyland adventures, going to Cook's Corner bar and others. How I wish we had so many more adventures together.

Chapter 14

Jen comes through

Brian Hurst was a British medium I had met many years earlier at a small group session in the home of Wanda Selling, a psychic who used to give me readings. Obviously, by this time I was well weaned away from my Jehovah's Witness upbringing. Some terrific evidence had come through Brian from my family members on the Other Side, and I booked a private session, hoping to hear from my dad.

Unfortunately, Brian was getting nothing on that very hot day. Thinking he was distracted by the noise of his fan, he tried shutting it off, but the heat was oppressive. Finally, he gave up and didn't charge me for the session.

Two weeks after losing Jennifer, Brian was the first medium I turned to. When I phoned to make the appointment, I told him only that my daughter had been killed, nothing more.

Rick went with me, and this time, our dad showed up loud and clear, along with Jen.

After chatting for a few minutes to hook into our energy, Brian said a prayer. He works with a spirit team, assisted by a spirit named Dr. Grant, who brings through the information from the Other Side.

"There appears to be a crime of passion here," Brian began. "Somebody said, 'If I can't have you, nobody else will.'"

That made sense. Then, "It looks to me like your daughter was on the verge of splitting up or wanting to break with this man who was very controlling ..."

"She was a girl who very much needed approval. She didn't have that much self-esteem deep down...she was nervous and somewhat uncertain of herself...You had an inkling, but you didn't know the whole story."

Brian went on to give a lot of evidence. He said he smelled liquor. I knew from the autopsy reports that both Jen and Tom were well over the legal limit for blood alcohol levels.

"The words were spoken, 'How could you do that to me?' There'd been one helluva fight.... I think the drink was making the speech excessively frank, even brutal. Who is Jenny, Jennifer?" I had not given him either of their names.

A few minutes later..."They keep saying 'Tom, Tom the piper's son, stole a pig and away did run."

Tom certainly did start to run away after he realized what he had done.

"Is this a gunshot?" Brian asked. "Apparently, he did something to her and he did something to himself....I feel like this man, he was just so crazed, he was drunk, and he was crazy....There's a lake somewhere. Something about a lake." They lived in Lake Forest.

"Jennifer has cleaned the slate because maybe in a past life she may have killed him. She used to have these awful rages, didn't she? And she'd scream and shout and throw things." It felt as if he knew her!

As the session went on, our dad started coming through. Rick and I both cracked up when Brian said, "He says he wouldn't come back here for all the tea in China." That was an expression Dad used all the time — 'for all the tea in China.' He'd regained his sense of humor on the Other Side.

When Brian started asking about someone named Rubinstein who worked in a store, Rick laughed in disbelief that he would get this information. Rick and Dad had worked together in a furniture store back in the '70s.

"We worked with a Mexican guy named Ruben," Rick explained. "As a joke, Dad would call him Ruben Stein."

Through Brian, Dad went on talking about things that would be meaningless to anyone else, but personal to Rick—how he'd dropped something heavy on his toe and nearly broke it and it got badly discolored. He talked about his stage days, too. Almost everything he said came in the form of a pun.

"I think he was a good man," Brian said. "I think he did his best. I think he made a few mistakes; no one is perfect. In his estimation you turned out to be decent people and he's proud of you."

There was much more, but even if these pieces of evidence that I've shared here had been all Brian had offered us, it would have brought tremendous comfort.

Chapter 15

Two more mediums

Three months after Jennifer's transition, Rick's wife told me about John Edward. He's famous now, having had a highly successful TV show called *Crossing Over with John Edward*. At that time, I hadn't heard of him. John is the author of one of my favorite afterlife books—*One Last Time*—which I recommend to anyone who wants to know about life after earth.

It was shortly before the TV show began to air, and John was on tour, promoting it. "He's going to be in L.A.," my sister-in-law urged, "You should go."

John was appearing at a hotel thirty miles south of where Bill and I lived. It wasn't until the afternoon of the event that I finally made up my mind to go.

After standing in a long line to buy my ticket, I found a seat towards the rear of the ballroom where John was to speak. Hundreds of people were there—probably close to a thousand—most of them hoping for messages from their dearly departed, and wanting to know what happens after we leave the earth.

John was late arriving. He had flown in from San Francisco and the airlines had lost his luggage, so he couldn't even change his clothes. Bounding into the room, he got up on stage feeling a little scattered, and began talking about his process.

"In a little while," he said, "some of your people will probably want to come through, and—" He stopped suddenly, mid-sentence, looking a little exasperated.

"Okay, someone is pushing to the head of the line and insisting on coming through *right now*." Looking over the assembled throng, he pointed to the side of the room where I sat. "On this side, towards the back. There's gunshots. It's a murder."

I stayed quiet, but a few rows behind me, a woman stood up and said, "It's my son."

John shook his head. "No. It's a daughter."

I looked around. Nobody was making a move, so I stood.

He started talking fast. "It happened in February. She knew who shot her. Two passed at the same time." After I acknowledged that he was correct, he said, "You had a dog that died?"

"No. I've never had a dog."

He cocked his head, listening to his spirit communicator, then said, "But you have a sister and she had a dog that died."

Yes! Wally, Sara's beloved Yellow Lab/Akita mix, had died the year before.

"Your daughter wants your sister to know that the dog is with her and he's fine."

For several minutes John went on giving accurate evidence about my dad's family, how they'd spoken two languages (Yiddish and English), and that dad had trouble with his legs and feet. And lots more. A week later, I learned that something he'd said was true, but I had been unaware of it. It involves someone else's private information, so sorry, I can't divulge it here.

I've seen claims John Edward researches the people he reads, which is patently ridiculous. I had showed up at the last minute, and in 2000 there was no Google. The personal things he told me were not something that would have been available to research.

⸎

A year and a half later I heard that producers of the *Beyond with James Van Praagh* TV show were inviting people to attend a taping. I went. They announced that James would be recording some shows in the homes of people who had stories to tell. I sent a letter with my story, and they picked me.

November 8, the day of the taping, was the day before my birthday and I believe that Jennifer had arranged it that way from the Other Side. James and his crew came to Bill's and my house. As he was walking through the door, James said, "Your father has been talking to me all the way here." Annoyingly, his producer jumped in and told him not to say anything more until the tape was 'rolling.'

Like John Edward, James talked about my father having a leg or foot problem. Then he said, "Your daughter is Jennifer, but she likes to be called Jen...Las Vegas, happier times." A few weeks after Tom and Jennifer met, they came to Bill's and my second wedding in Las Vegas.

"She was in between jobs when she was killed." True.

"Tell her father she is okay and not to beat himself up." Actually, I thought he *should* beat himself up. But, I'm not as spiritually evolved as James Van Praagh.

"She was rushed to the hospital; you almost lost her then." I assume that referred to the 5150 mental health hold.

"When she was killed, she was seeing two men." That would be Tom and Scott. "There was a breakup; running away."

"She says she was screaming but no one came to help." That makes me think of her calling 911 and no one showing up until it was too late."

James said something pretty funny: "Your mother thinks you are evil, but you're not." If my mother had known I had invited a psychic medium into my house she would have fainted.

"Something about one of your sons and popcorn," James said.

Erik had recently burned some in the microwave and stunk up the house. Apparently, Jen could smell it from the Other Side.

After the session was over and the crew was packing up to leave, I started to say to James, "There's a doll on the shelf above my desk—"

"Did it fall?" he interrupted.

"Yes."

"It was Jen who made it jump."

Chapter 16

Here comes baby

One thing I learned from my first pregnancy is, if you eat a cheese sandwich with a glass of whole milk almost every day for nine months, you'll gain forty pounds. Well, that's what happened to me, anyway. I had started at a slender 125.

In late 1972 when our first child was born, Ken and I had been married for three years, and not happily. A week after the wedding he was accusing me of planting sewing pins in the carpet to hurt him when he was doing his workout. It didn't get better from there. I foolishly thought that a baby was the solution to our problems. Or maybe I didn't consciously think that. I just wanted someone to love who would love me back.

I'd had a miscarriage in the first year and couldn't seem to get pregnant again. My doctor, Howard Marchbanks, prescribed Clomid, a fertility drug, and had me take my temperature every day. Nope, nothing happening. Until, finally, after an outpatient procedure, he phoned and said, "Hang onto your head, honey, you're pregnant!"

OMG, we were having a baby!!! I was sewing maternity clothes almost before I hung up the phone.

The baby was due at the end of November, but it was the 23rd, the day before Thanksgiving, when I went into labor. The contractions were more than Braxton-Hicks 'practice' ones, but they weren't yet strong enough and close enough together to keep me home. Obviously, I would not be cooking a turkey dinner on the holiday, so I went to the grocery store and got the fixings for a big pot of chili and cornbread. That was dinner handled for the next couple of days.

To the chagrin of the medical establishment who hounded him for years for being unconventional, Dr. Marchbanks believed that hospitals were for sick people and most babies should be born at home. Along with a midwife, he successfully delivered hundreds of infants that way all over Orange County. The midwife was Jane Woods, an Amazon better known as Woody. She delivered two of my three babies, but she had Thanksgiving off and wasn't present for the first one. The doctor was on his own.

By the time I'd cooked the chili and cornbread, made sure the apartment was clean and presentable, and got the few supplies ready for the birth (don't I sound like a pioneer woman?!) the contractions were much stronger and closer together. It turned out I was having back labor, which means the hard back of the baby's head was pressing against my spine. Wouldn't you know, that makes for a longer and more painful than normal labor.

Shoot. Why can't I do things the normal way?

After midnight the pain intensified. Ken, who was unable to sleep with my moaning and groaning, strongly suggested I take myself to the living room. I had taken Bradley childbirth classes (on my own), but you're supposed to have a partner to remind you to do the breathing exercises. I curled up on the couch and tried to find a comfortable position. On my back. On my side. On my knees, in downward dog.

Feeling alone and scared, I held out until 2:00 a.m.

It was easy to see why Dr. Marchbanks' patients were so smitten with him. Unlike my partner in the bedroom, he was kind and gentle, and as far as I could tell, not annoyed at being woken in the wee hours. Maybe having nine children of his own and five marriages had taught him patience. He talked me through some contractions and promised to check on me in the morning.

In 1972, there were no extravagant gender reveal parties with pink or blue smoke/balloons/cupcakes to tell expectant parents what color baby clothes to buy. They had to wait and learn the gender with an actual in-person gander. But I knew. I had read an (old wives tale) article that said if the baby's heart rate was fast—over 140 bpm it's a girl. Below 140 bpm, a boy. Since my baby's heart rate hovered around 138—Dr. Marchbanks' nurse gave me a cassette tape of it—that was all I needed to know. There wasn't a scintilla of doubt in my mind: we were having a boy.

So, it's Thanksgiving Day. Everything is ready. The crib is painted yellow and set up in the second bedroom, spread with a crocheted baby blanket made by yours truly. Piles of adorable clothes—loot from no less than three baby showers—neatly folded in dresser drawers, waiting to be worn. Desitin, not talc, is ready to keep the tiny bottom dry. A Sesame Street mobile hangs above the crib, giving baby something interesting and brain-stimulating to look at.

Soon after my wedding, my mother had taken my little brother Richard and moved to the Deep South to do missionary work, so she was not with us to welcome her first grandchild. Ken's parents arrived in the afternoon. Since Jehovah's Witnesses don't recognize any secular or religious holidays there was no turkey dinner to interrupt at their house. Notably, however, JWs do think it prudent to take advantage of holiday sale prices, so they'll buy a turkey or two for later consumption—when it won't look like they're celebrating the holiday. Like, the day after. Seriously.

We can always find ways to justify the things we want to do.

Dr. Marchbanks was unlucky enough to get called away from his holiday feast to our apartment in Santa Ana—the life of an OB doc. Upon arriving around 3:00, he checked on the baby's progress. Because labor had been going on for so long, he broke my water, after which, things moved fairly quickly and our firstborn burst into the world.

At 5:30 p.m. precisely two weeks after my twenty-third birthday, Dr. Marchbanks made the announcement with a big smile. "Well, honey, looks like your boy is a girl."

What? Did he say a *girl?*

Chapter 17
She wasn't always Jennifer

Yep. Seven-pounds, four-ounces with straight black hair that would curl over the first few weeks. A baby girl with a strong pair of lungs that brought her into the world red-faced and screaming.

Maybe she regretted from the beginning coming into this life.

The jolt that she was she and not he didn't lessen the thrill of meeting our daughter and confirming that she had arrived safely, all with the right number of fingers and toes. Ken's beaming face in one of the Polaroids my father-in-law took is a favorite. He didn't even complain about missing his favorite TV rerun, *The Wild Wild West,* which came on at that time.

Ken's opening bid for a name had been Kratos because, he said, it sounded tough. I took it seriously then, but I have to wonder if he was just pushing my buttons. When I uttered a resounding No, his older sister suggested Kendra, which would be okay now, when babies have all sorts of names, like Apple or Cinnamon. Or Kendra. But back then, more traditional names were the norm.

I wanted to call her Jennifer. Ken didn't.

Finally, we compromised. That is, I compromised. My husband was a fan of two singers with the same name: *Bonnie* Raitt and *Bonnie* Bramlett (of Delaney and Bonnie).

That didn't land much better with me than Kratos. In my junior year of high school, my home economics teacher was named Bonnie Jean Jones. I suppose she had a reason for taking a dislike to me, and I didn't like her, either. When I was assigned to her room again the next year, even before she said, "Are *you* in here again?" the dismay was plain on her face.

Frankly, I don't think anything I did was rotten enough to deserve that kind of reaction, and it left a bad taste. I didn't want to use her name for my baby. But with Bonnie being the *only* name we could halfway agree on, I caved.

As fate would have it, both Ken's and my mother were named Elizabeth, and that was how the name on her birth certificate came to be Bonnie Elizabeth Lowe. She never knew the story of how she got the name Bonnie, or that I wanted to call her Jennifer, and yet, she grew up hating her name. Just yesterday, I had a reading with a phenomenal astrologer and psychic medium named Lisa Salvatore, who, mid-reading asked if my daughter had a name other than Jennifer. When I said that her birth name was Bonnie, she immediately said, "and she hated that name!"

I always knew it was the wrong name for her.

In her early twenties Bonnie renamed herself to—drum roll please—Jennifer. Yes, really. It seems that on some level, we both always knew that was supposed to be her name.

And yet, after all those years of calling her Bonnie I found it hard to change and call her Jennifer, which ticked her off. A lot. I get it—I didn't like my name either, and in eighth grade tried to get people to call me Shelly, but it never took. Aside from my best friend, only my nerdy math teacher ever called me that, and he was more than a little bit creepy.

Bonnie was twenty-six when she applied for a legal name change. Two weeks before she was killed, it came through, so the name on her death certificate and her headstone is Jennifer Elizabeth Lowe. Now it's hard to think of her as ever being named anything else.

Chapter 18

Things go south

When she was nine months old, Bonnie fell out of her crib. She had been napping and I'll never know how, as I was always careful with it, but the side of the crib came down and she landed on the carpet, screaming. There were no visible injuries and when I called the doctor he said there was nothing to be done, just watch her.

At first, she seemed okay. But after a couple of months, I started noticing changes in her behavior. She'd had bad colic through her first six weeks of life, but now there were uncontrollable fits, where she would just scream. Every. Day. Nothing helped, except to give her a bottle. I had breast fed her until the milk dried up when she was three months old and Dr. Marchbanks said, "You've made a valiant effort, but it's time to give up." He put her on soy formula and I felt like a failure.

Over time, as the screaming fits grew into hideous tantrums, I took her to one doctor after another, but none had a solution. One pediatrician helpfully (not) told me I was a battered woman. In the sense of emotional battering he was right, but it would be a long time before I was ready to see that.

Bonnie turned two and started avoiding her bedroom. She would frequently say, "There's a goose in my room," and refuse to enter. Now, more than forty years and a lot of experience later, I ask myself, was she actually saying, "ghost" and not "goose?" And if so, who had it been?

Many small children have paranormal experiences that scare them. Some remember events from past lives. My friend Judith's little granddaughter used to tell her that she, the child, used to be the mother and that she died in a fire. Usually by the age of around six, they get involved in the activities of daily life and begin to forget.

Bonnie turned three, then four, and the tantrums continued. If I refused to give her a bottle, she would lie on the floor, screeching to scare a banshee, and pushing herself around on her back, following me wherever I went. I was ready and willing to not give in to her toddler terrorist demands. If she wore herself out and didn't get that bottle, surely she would get the message and give it up. But it wasn't that easy.

Her father demanded that I make her stop the racket whatever it took, or he would take over—a threat I could not risk. This was a daily scene until she was five. I guess she finally realized that she was too big to be carrying a baby bottle around.

Then it was time for kindergarten. Ken didn't want her to go, and argued against her starting school until it was the middle of the school year. Our daughter was a very smart little cookie who had learned to read more than fifty words before she was two. I'd read *How to Teach Your Baby To Read* and their method worked really well. However, when she finally entered kindergarten, as a left-hander she had some challenges learning to write and draw.

It wasn't until after years of serious emotional problems that a psychologist who tested her at ten years of age concluded that Bonnie was exhibiting symptoms of a closed head injury: personality change, trouble with concentration, and so on. Her behavior became so extreme—she threatened her younger brother Erik with a kitchen knife—that she was referred to a psychiatrist who suggested a residential children's behavioral program. By then, I was divorced and desperate to get help for my daughter. I had two little boys to care for as well, and much of the time was working three low-paying part-time jobs to feed and clothe them.

The day she was to be admitted to Charter Oak Hospital I picked her up from Monte Vista Elementary School. On the way out to the car, Bonnie was mouthing off in the loud and embarrassing way she often did. One of the other mothers walked by, staring openmouthed. "How can you let her talk to you that way?" she exclaimed, aghast.

I wanted to yell at her, "You have no idea what I've been going through; what I'm about to go through. Do you think I *want* her to talk to me that way? Do you think I want my child to be hospitalized?"

Maybe if I could have said that out loud she would have had some compassion. Or maybe not. I clamped my mouth shut and walked away without answering.

That experience gave me greater empathy for people whose situations I might otherwise have looked at askance. If we could remind ourselves that we don't know what is behind another's actions and give them the benefit of the doubt, the world would be a kinder place.

Over the three months Bonnie was a patient, I attended a parent support group at the hospital every Tuesday evening. It was a place for us to share our fears and concerns with the therapist who led the group. I listened to some of the stories, appalled at what some of these kids had gone through.

The twelve-year-old blind boy whose father had shot everyone in the family and killed them all except him. The bullet had pierced his brain and severed his optic nerve, but the boy lived and was subsequently molested by a caregiver. He was in the residential program for inappropriate sexual behavior. No duh.

There was a six-year-old girl who was experiencing hallucinations. The doctors were talking about a diagnosis of schizophrenia and committing her to Camarillo State Hospital; a nightmare. I wonder now whether she was actually seeing spirit.

And the girl whose father was so controlling that when she didn't get up on time, he made her go to school in her pajamas. And when she didn't want to eat, force fed her until she vomited. After which, he made her collect the vomit in a bowl and pour it on herself, then sit in the sun until it baked.

Don't judge me too harshly when I tell you that I had to get that father's handwriting samples—his ex-wife, the girl's mother, attended the group; he did not. And yes, his handwriting was as brutal as you might expect it to be.

I have wondered whatever happened to those children, who are now in their fifties.

The months Bonnie spent at Charter Oak were a guilty respite for me. The times I would go to visit her and she would be rude and nasty, I turned and walked away, relieved that someone else had to deal with her behavior. And yet, walking away from my ten-year-old child was agonizing and felt like another failure.

Over time, she actually enjoyed being in the program—they had video games! She began to make improvements and we got closer. For a while anyway.

Chapter 19

Why not?

Ken and I were attracted to each other as young teenagers. We moved in the same JW social circles, and started dating when I was sixteen and he was nearly nineteen. We shared our poetry. I'm happy to admit he was a much better poet than I. He was (is), in fact, brilliant. He always beat me at chess, except once. That was the last time we played. Despite his JW upbringing and being appointed as an elder, Ken became a chemist and a sought-after consultant.

Most of that came after me, though.

Ken is African American, I am Caucasian. We adopted the motto, "Why not?"

When we started dating there was a statute on the books in Anaheim, where I lived, which said people of color could not be within the city limits after sundown (yes, in the late 1960s!). Sundown towns, as they were known, were all-white neighborhoods that openly practiced racism. When I lived there I never knew that the KKKs presence in Anaheim earned it the moniker, "Klanaheim." Ken and his family lived in Placentia, a good area and not as white as an alligator's underbelly.

Interracial marriage was still uncommon in those days, even in California. Just three years after Loving v. Virginia was argued at the US Supreme Court, in which interracial marriage became legal in the U.S., Ken's twin brother and his white wife were the first interracial couple to live in Anaheim. They had a nice apartment (but it was on an alley).

Ken noticed the stares more than I ever did. But one day racism hit me in the face.

We had been visiting his parents and were driving home in his '68 Cobra Jet 428 limited edition Mustang—only 50 of them were made. Many a Friday and Saturday evening were spent at Lyon's Drag Strip in Long Beach, or Irwindale Raceway. His drag racing trophy was on prominent display in our living room. Some years after he sold it for twice what he'd paid (which wouldn't amount to a down payment on today's cars) his brother Doug told us he saw our car—white with a black hood scoop—in *Hot Rod* magazine, valued at north of $80,000. I've recently been told it would now be worth about three times that much.

Back to the story...we were near our apartment in Santa Ana when we got pulled over by a cop for DWB: Driving While Black. Having spotted my pale face in the passenger seat, the cop just wanted to know if I was "okay."

On another occasion, Ken was riding his *bicycle* mid-morning and got stopped for 'intent to speed.'

Experiences such as those, and later, bigotry experienced by our children, offered me a different perspective on how people of color are forced to be constantly on the alert. One of Ken's early poems put it succinctly:

A white dog
Bit a black dog
100 years later
They are still fighting

The sad fact is, though, we had problems before we were married and they continued to grow afterwards. These were not racially based issues, but more on the order of personality differences that would, over the course of time, destroy our relationship.

I had grown up in a broken home and was emotional and headstrong. He had grown up with strict disciplinarian parents and was jealous and, in my view, paranoid. A minor incident occurred when I was sixteen and a group of us teens went to the local pool hall—a decent one, not a dive. I rode in Ken's car. During the evening, joking around, I sat on our friend, Chet's lap. After that night, for all the years we were together—all throughout our marriage—I never heard the end of that 'betrayal.'

Stuff like that.

I didn't know how to read the road signs. Like this one: Shortly before we were to get married Ken informed me that he and his mother had gone shopping and bought the furniture for the apartment we had just rented. His mother and I got along fine, but I have to wonder how either of them thought it was okay to exclude me from that shopping trip. At the same time, though, it didn't occur to me that something was wrong with this picture.

Six years earlier, my dad, on a pretext, had dumped my mother, brother, and me at my grandmother's house in England. He claimed to have a job interview in the north and would be back in two days. He didn't come back.

On borrowed money, and over my strong protests, my mother took us back to the US in pursuit of her husband. I don't know how she managed it, but she rented a two-bedroom apartment for $85/month. Having sold everything in our move to England, we had nothing but our clothes. Zip. Zilch. Zero.

The Anaheim congregation we attended—the same JW friends we had said goodbye to several months earlier—chipped in with various bits and pieces to furnish the place.

To make ends meet—and it took some real stretching to get those ends to meet—we got a piano and Mum taught the children of the 'brothers' and 'sisters' in the congregation. It's worth noting that the folks who had the least to give who offered us the nicest stuff, while those who had much—well, maybe that uncomfortable horsehair sofa was actually worth a lot and we just didn't realize its value. All I know is, it made my bare legs itch.

There was a really cool old sideboard, and an unfinished flip-top desk that I immediately commandeered and painted white with green swirls. Or maybe it was green with white swirls. I did a lot of painting in those days. The walls were continually changing color.

I have concluded this is why, when I learned that without my input, new bedroom and living room furniture was to be delivered on our wedding day, my attitude was grateful and excited, rather than miffed.

♪

Another important road sign I missed was Ken's insistence that our engagement be kept secret...because it was nobody's business. The wedding, such as it was, was held in our apartment on Wednesday evening, October 1, 1969. Ken's parents, my mother, and the JW minister who performed the ceremony and his wife were the only guests. My dad, my little brother, Ken's twin, and their other siblings were not informed until the next day, when it was a *fait accompli*.

We had a nice little wedding cake. I wore a dress I'd made myself when I was a bridesmaid at a friend's wedding. My deer-in-the-headlights stare in the photo my new father-in-law took proved prophetic.

My mother had strongly advocated for me to marry Ken despite the misgivings I had—he didn't always treat me well when we were dating. She was his champion, his cheerleader. And, at nearly twenty, a JW girl was looked upon almost as an old maid who needed to become some man's submissive wife.

For a time, my mother and Ken were 'pioneer partners.' Pioneering requires a commitment to spend a minimum 100 hours a month in unpaid ministry work. The two of them must have knocked on thousands of doors together, taking the message of the Kingdom to the neighborhood, whether householders wanted to hear it or not; conducting free Bible studies in people's homes, and giving talks on the Ministry School at one of the three meetings we were expected to attend every week. Non-pioneer members were supposed to meet or exceed a quota of ten hours a month for the same activities.

In the mid-late 1960s the Vietnam war was raging, and at the end of 1969 the Selective Service System held its first lottery drawing since 1942. This was not a fun lottery where you win a million billion bucks. This was the military Draft where young men were assigned a random number between 1 and 366 that corresponded to their birthday. Lower numbers were called up first, which according to the government website, meant that the first men (boys, really) drafted would turn 20 during the calendar year of the lottery.

Jehovah's Witnesses do not believe in going to war. The military allowed people they designated Conscientious Objectors to serve in the armed forces in a noncombatant capacity. That didn't work for JWs. Alternative service was not allowed.

During WWII, because of their refusal to serve, some Jehovah's Witnesses in the Deep South were tarred and feathered. And if that's not a term you've heard, it means a mob strips the person naked, smears them with hot tar, and covers them with bird feathers.

You might not agree with the decision not to serve, but if you can imagine what happens to skin treated this way, I expect you will agree it's a barbaric form of torture.

Many of the young JW men I knew began to pioneer in the hopes of receiving a 4-D classification, which would designate them a minister and allow them to avoid the Draft. Not everyone who applied was approved, and our friends who were not were called draft dodgers and sent to prison for two years. They served their sentence, were released and, when they remained steadfast in their refusal to go to war, were returned for two more years of incarceration.

Ken had a deferment for health reasons, but we were constantly in fear that his number might come up anyway. I dreaded going to pick up the mail each day in case a letter came from the Selective Service System.

He chose to become a pioneer and work part-time—it's what was expected by the 'governing body' of the religion. Rather than seek higher education or a lucrative career, especially the young Witnesses were pressured to engage in the full-time ministry. Those who did pursue a secular career were looked down upon as being 'worldly,' rather than spiritual.

Being worldly was not a good thing.

Those who took up the unpaid labor of pioneering still had to feed their families and pay the bills. Fulfilling that 100 hour/month commitment meant getting a part time job, usually cleaning houses or offices, window washing, or gardening. The Congregation Servant (head elder) of the Ana-heim congregation—Billy B. Schmidt, who we privately dubbed the Big Bee—employed several young men in his agronomy (gardening) business, including Ken. Last I checked, his son, Billy D, was still at it.

For my mother, who was completely devoted to the religion to the exclu-sion of all else, pioneering was a logical step. I had been a latchkey kid as a child in England while she worked, and Richard and I were latchkey kids together while her afternoons were spent at other people's homes, teaching them JW beliefs.

Soon after I got married, my mother took Richard and moved to Mississip-pi and Louisiana. We had friends who had moved there and when the gov-erning body identified those places as an area where "the need was greater," (to proselytize), she jumped on the opportunity to serve as a missionary.

Chapter 20

Learning to be abused

If you saw a baby left outdoors by the babysitter on freezing winter days, would you tell its mother? Our neighbors did, but it didn't do me any good.

Science tells us that sensory memory, such as taste, links to another memory. That explains why, as I write these words, that thanks to abusive treatment by my babysitter, the nasty medicine I had to take for frequent earaches and a perforated eardrum is once again on my tongue.

Until I was three, we lived in a place called Debden, not far from London, where I was born. The only memory I have of Debden is playing in big clods of dirt with a girl named Judy who had a plastic knife with a red handle. According to *Wikipedia* it's a lovely village with a current population of 780.

Mrs. Gosling was the neighbor who watched me while my mother worked as a telephone operator—a job that made her miserable. Neighbors reported to her that I was being shut in a dark cupboard when I fussed, and was often left outdoors in my pram, my screams going unheeded.

Enough times to burn it into my memory, My mother told me as I was growing up, "I went to work crying every day because I had to leave you with that horrible Mrs. Gosling."

In knowing that I was being abused and continuing to leave me with my abuser, the message she transmitted was, you can cry about it, but you just have to suck it up and take it. Her words sowed the seed that grew into a Very Bad Habit of staying in abusive situations for far too long. I understand that she was reacting out of her own life experiences and didn't know any better, but I'm not sure that's a good enough excuse. That said, I take responsibility for passing the same bad message on to my own children through my behavior.

Seven years since WWII ended and I arrived on earth we left Debden and moved to a post-war two-bedroom flat in Islington, a borough of London. I hear it's quite toney now. In 1953, it wasn't.

The flats, called Isledon House, formed a large triangle over an entire block, with a grassy area in the middle that I was never allowed to play on. That entire area had been a victim of the Blitz during 1940-41, as well as a target for rocket attacks in 1944. So much of London was destroyed that it took a long time to clear away the debris and rebuild.

There was a playground near our flats, but my friends and I had to cross a bomb site to get to it. Once we did, we'd do all of the stuff kids have always done—swing as high as we could on the swings, and spin as fast as we could on the roundabout (merry-go-round). The slide was so tall, I was afraid to climb up it.

The bomb site, having been reduced to rubble and not yet rebuilt, was a treasure trove for kids under ten. A chair with its springs sticking out of the seat; other bits and pieces of furniture and miscellaneous rubbish. I have a vivid memory of finding half a big jawbone—presumably from an animal. I can still picture it with teeth jutting out.

December 29, 1953 was my introduction to Spirit. In the middle of the night, I climbed out of bed and went to the living room. My parents found me sitting alone on the couch.

"What are you doing out here?" they asked.

With four-year-old innocence I looked up at them and said, "Grandpa died."

The next day, my father learned that his dad, my Grandpa Max, had died of a heart attack at 73. That's the age I am as I write these words. It feels too young.

How could I have known that Grandpa had died? Where had the information come from? Had Grandpa stopped off to say goodbye to me on his way to the Other Side? That's what I believe.

I was even younger—three—when I woke up one night from a terrifying dream that all these years later remains clear in my mind. I was frantically running around an orangey-yellow bowl-shaped arena being chased, and finally eaten, by a lion.

Could this have been a past life memory as a martyred Christian in Roman times? There is so much we don't know.

Chapter 21

Culture clash

My parents met while performing in pantomime theatre, and got married six weeks later in a registry office, with two of their cast mates as witnesses. In England pantomime is most often a Christmas stage production of a fairytale such as Snow White, Little Red Riding Hood, or Dick Whittington and his Cat. Think slapstick comedy, music, and standup.

My dad, born Israel ("Issy") Schneider (do I need to say he was Jewish?), changed his name for the stage to its literal translation, Peter Taylor (his father was a journeyman tailor). My mother, born Elizabeth Ahrens, took her mother's maiden name and became Vicky King. She was raised Church of England. This was a disaster in the making.

My *shiksa* mother was eager to impress her new husband's family, but completely ignorant of Jewish food restrictions (and everything else Jewish). Apparently, she had no clue that serving pork pie to Jews was not a good idea. I have to wonder why dad evidently didn't educate her.

Although Dad's family was not at all religious, my aunts, Pearlie, Minnie, and Rosie got on their high horse and refused to come to the table. Grandpa Max, though, did. The pie, as my mother tells it, was mostly crust with a bit of sausage down the middle, but Grandpa not only ate it, he complimented his daughter-in-law. Long after she and his son split up, my mother thought of him with love, and remained touched by his kindness to a naive young woman.

The three sisters, who wanted to protect their younger brother, predicted that the marriage wouldn't last a month. They were off by fourteen years, but they did come to accept my mother into the family. I'm glad they did, as Aunty Rosie made the best strudel ever.

My maternal grandparents were lovely people, but had a slight edge of snob to them. Grandad Ahrens told my dad, "We like you Pete, but don't come around too often." Dad used to make a joke of it, but how could that not have wounded him?

When Pete and Vicky met, she was already the mother of a six-week-old infant. She had been seduced by a fifty-year-old man, another performer in a different show. He dosed her with silver nitrate, a toxic chemical meant to induce abortion. In her case, it didn't.

The baby, my half-sister Jean Susan was born gravely ill a year and a week before me. The doctors diagnosed leukemia, and she died at eight months of age. I am grateful my parents took photos of her beautiful little smiling face.

Sometimes when I have readings with mediums, she comes through as an adult to say she is with me.

Things were different in 1948. My grandfather took my mother to stay at an unwed mother's home to await the birth. As he said goodbye on the doorstep, for the first time she could remember, her dad hugged her and told her he loved her.

To rush into a marriage to a relative stranger with a baby, Dad must have been uber infatuated. Overweight as he was, and with a ring of Friar Tuck hair on his otherwise bald head, it may have been my mother's need for someone to take care of her and Jean Susan that initially attracted her. Whether that is the case or not, for a long time, she did love him, and he loved her, too.

Chapter 22

Pete Taylor

My dad was sickly as a child, and the doctors sent him to a sanatorium for several weeks. Once he was discharged and went home, he started gaining weight—a lot of it—and losing his hair. Thyroid problems. And then...

You know how your parents always warned you against running with a sharp stick? Playing a dangerous game with neighborhood kids, young Issy was partially blinded in one eye. In all the years I knew him I never questioned why he had one brown eye and one a hazy blue. He was just Dad.

His mother, my Grandma Eva, who I never knew, died when he was fourteen. She was in her early 50s when her heart gave out. Both she and Grandpa Max were originally born in Poland, and somewhere around WWI immigrated from Minsk in Belarus to England with a daughter, Pearl, and a son, Beinis. In England, Minnie and Rosie were added to the family, and finally, Israel. I've been told there were two other daughters, Miriam and Ruby, who died in Russia.

Evil stepmothers are an ongoing theme in my family. After Grandma died, Grandpa, who must have needed help with all those kids, remarried. His new wife and Issy (another family theme—changing one's name) didn't get along, and she kicked him out of the house the moment she could get away with it.

In 1939 when war broke out in England, Issy wanted to serve. Despite his experience in boxing and wrestling he didn't match the physical/health profile for the British Army. And there was that partial blindness thing. He was, however, deemed fit enough to drive a lorry (British for truck), so that's what he did during the war.

When the war ended he changed his name to Peter Taylor and signed on with Jack Lewis' all-male revue, *This Was the Army*. US audiences would call it vaudeville. Or maybe a drag show. I wish he was still around for me to ask how that all came about.

When I was four or five they took me to see him perform.

One of Dad's 'bits' was a ridiculous little poem that made me giggle every time he recited it:

> *I wish I was a little pig,*
> *no porky could be flasher.*
> *I'd take my little curly tail*
> *and tickle me gammon rasher.*

Little me stood in the aisle of the huge, dark theater, fascinated to see a double-jointed man called 'Arthur Knotto' literally tie himself in knots. With his wide forehead and receding hairline, he looked a bit like Fred Astaire. He was a witness at my parents' wedding.

All of the cast members were army veterans, and all performed in drag—Sonny Dawkes was the most glam of them all (Google him). Photos of my rotund dad show him playing, variously, a washerwoman, a pirate, a robber, and a soldier.

From a newspaper article I cherish:

> "The knockabout comedy is extreme-
> ly well done...Jack Lewis is aided and
> abetted by Arthur Turner, a wonderful
> Dame Trot, and James Regan and Pete
> Taylor as the two robbers. *The latter is a*

wonderful character and almost steals the whole show." Proud italics mine.

Dad was always joking and being silly before his first stroke—before his personality changed and he got very quiet. When I was little, he also did a lot of shouting, which was typically how his family communicated. Polar opposite was my mother's British stiff upper lip family. I don't think I ever heard one of them raise their voice.

Chapter 23

Elizabeth Ahrens

The stage had always drawn my mother. She was nearly fourteen when she ran away to sing and dance professionally.

She and my aunt were named for the princesses. My mother was Elizabeth, or Betty at home, and Margaret, known as Molly. Aunty Molly has told me about the wonderful shows her big sister put on with the neighborhood kids.

Much like her first granddaughter, Bonnie/Jennifer, Betty was a rebellious child, impossible to control. She was not 'bad,' but she had a strong mind of her own. I know from personal experience what a mixed blessing that can be.

When her parents didn't know what to do with her anymore, at the grand old age of six, Betty was shipped off to a convent boarding school. The nuns there failed to whip her into shape and expelled her. Another school followed; another expulsion. Wash, rinse, repeat.

She must have been eleven or twelve when she played truant from class one day, and snuck into the village for an ice cream cornet (cone to US readers). Spying a teacher, she stuffed her ice cream into her handbag and hurried back to school. Imagine the melty mess by the time she opened it later. All in all, a pretty harmless escapade.

There were less pleasant tales of the convent school. Pupils were required to kneel and kiss the feet of a Jesus figure nailed to a wall-mounted crucifix. One of the girls wasn't fast enough and a nun gave her head a shove forward. It must have been a hard shove, as the nail in Jesus' feet pierced her lip. Personally, I doubt that Jesus himself would have approved. Watching that atrocious episode left an impression on young Betty Ahrens.

After one too many expulsions, Betty became Vicky King, singer and chorus girl. According to my aunt, her parents knew where she was and didn't
bring her home. They were okay with her doing her thing.

She was sixteen when she won a role in a show featuring twelve-year-old
Petula Clark, who sang "Sweet Little Alice Blue Gown." She also performed
in a show starring Benny Hill.

It sometimes seemed as if my mother had a bit of Lucille Ball in her. Like
her tale of a dance routine that went hilariously wrong. She was dancing in
the chorus line doing her high kicks with the rest of the girls, when the zipper
on her skimpy satin shorts broke. Gravity being what it is, the shorts started
to drop.

She could have gracefully slipped behind the curtains, but Vicky, deciding
that the show must go on, ignored the dance mistress, who was hissing at her
to get offstage, and clung to her shorts. She held them together and kept on
kicking.

To the audience's delight, the shorts kept dropping and she kept dancing.
By the time the routine was over and the music died, everyone except the
dance mistress and a red-faced Vicky King were howling with laughter.

Until long after I was born, she continued as a fan dancer and a ballet
dancer, too. I would watch in awe as she transformed for a performance of
Swan Lake. The next day, I was allowed to wear her pink toe shoes and tutu,
and the soft white feathers that covered her ears.

I thought I wanted to learn ballet, so she took me to Saddlers Wells ballet
school in London. We were shown into the practice studio where a class of
little girls my age were doing Pliés at the barre. My mother tried to usher me
into the group. It must have been a disappointment when I hid behind her
skirt, too shy to join in. Thenceforth, my Pirouettes and Grande Jetés were
confined to our living room.

My cousins, Pat and Jenny, came home from living in Egypt and when they brought a real fez and tales of life in the desert, I could not have been more impressed. My interest in being a ballerina was quickly replaced by a fascination for Ancient Egypt that has never left me.

Don't worry, I don't believe I was Cleopatra or Nefertiti in a past life. Several psychics have, of their own accord, told me I was a scribe. Could my lifelong sleep apnea have its roots in a past life in Egypt? I imagine myself in the household of a high-ranking master who, as punishment for displeasing his pharaoh, the entire household is buried alive...Never mind. I'll stick to mystery writing.

I have a feeling that once she quit performing, my mother missed it. She had a beautiful singing voice and could often be heard belting out *The Sunny Side of the Street*—which she called her signature tune—as she danced around our flat.

Whenever she did something that went wrong, she would get that wide-eyed Lucille Ball look of innocence. "But Pete," she would protest, "It just came off in my hand." (whatever 'it' was).

For example, I was (luckily) sitting on the windowsill playing with my paper dolls when she managed to blow up the pressure cooker. Dad, still the comedian in those days, got a big kick out of teasing her and joking about the many silly things she did.

It's a shame she became a religious fanatic and stopped being fun.

Chapter 24

Nanny and the Spirits

My grandmother, Elsie Ahrens, lived to be eighty-eight. She'd dealt with a number of major health problems throughout her life, including breast cancer in her late forties, which resulted in a radical mastectomy and cobalt treatments.

Recuperating meant spending a significant amount of time in bed. On at least one occasion, she reported seeing a beautiful white hand floating above her. Far from being frightened, she welcomed the contact from Spirit.

Early on, exploring her interest in spiritualism, Nanny invited a spiritualist couple to the house. They were good, kind people, but my mother, then four years old, was petrified. I'm told she hid under the table, refusing to come out until the visit ended and they left the house.

What makes it all the stranger is that while at boarding school, my mother and her friends played with a Ouija board once, with hair-raising results.

They were laughing and making fun of the 'game,' when suddenly, an unseen force wrenched the planchette out of their hands and launched it across the room, where it smashed against the wall. And as if that wasn't enough to scare the bejezus out of a group of teens, the heavy wardrobe that held their clothes jumped away from the wall as if an earthquake had hit. After that incident, my mother's fear of Spirit never left her.

My grandmother's interest in the spirit world continued. When she and Grandad sold their house, *Vraucourt,* to their older son, my Uncle Roy, their new home had an unusual feature—bronze grip bars were attached to the downstairs walls at waist height. There were occasions when Nanny saw an elderly lady with a cane walking around the house. She invited the vicar to tea and asked him about it.

"Oh, that's Mrs. Green," said the vicar casually, as if seeing spirits was an everyday occurrence. "She died here." The grip bars had been installed to help the disabled elderly lady to make her way around the house.

After the so-called Great War, which killed upward of twenty million, many of the people left behind were desperate to know what goes on after we leave our life on the earth. Where were their loved ones, they wanted to know? What were they doing? High-profile people like Arthur Conan Doyle, whose son was a casualty of WWI, and whose wife was herself a medium, led serious research in matters of the Afterlife.

Only recently, I learned that one of my grandfather's brothers, Reginald Ahrens ("Uncle Reg"), was a member of a spiritualist church on the Isle of Wight. I haven't been able to find out much about him, except that he had a rep for being a bit of an oddball. For one thing, he wore a full suit and tie at the beach, which seems pretty mild. But goodness knows what else. My aunt remembers him living with Grandad and family at Vraucourt during WWII. He kept mostly to himself, sleeping on a cot in the hallway and interacting little with the rest of the family.

I've tried contacting one of the spiritualists churches on the Isle of Wight in the hope that might have old membership rolls with Reg's name on it. So far, my efforts have been unsuccessful.

One morning soon after Jennifer crossed to the spirit world, I was at my doctor's office waiting to be seen. Wandering over to the large windows in his second-floor suite I looked down at the parking lot, thinking about the spirit world.

People were walking to and from their cars, blithely going about their business. None of them had a clue that they were being watched by someone who was unable to communicate with them through the glass.

Suddenly, I got the oddest sense that this is what it's like for those on the Other Side—that the people we love who have crossed over can see us, but it's not easy for them to reach out and let us know they are there. If I had rapped on the window, it's possible that someone might have looked up and seen me. Otherwise, I was invisible. And yet, I existed.

Chapter 25
Early days

Touring got to be too much for Mum and Dad. Or possibly, my grandparents couldn't cope with a small child who was left with them for weeks at a time. I didn't mind at all staying with Nanny and Granddad. I especially loved it when Nanny got her kitchen scale out of the pantry and let me weigh up the sugar and flour to 'help' her make butterfly cakes. What I actually helped make was a huge (and delicious) mess.

In the course of time, my parents quit showbiz and found 'serious' jobs to pay the bills. More than sixty years later I still remember how much Mum loathed her supervisor, Miss Neller, at the telephone company where she was an operator. Anyone old enough to remember Lily Tomlin's character, Ernestine ("Is this the party to whom I am speaking?"), that was my mother, pushing wired plugs into a switchboard, with the power to connect and disconnect calls. A far cry from mobile phones.

Dad drove a coach (equivalent to a charter bus). Sometimes he would be hired to take a group to the circus, and took me with him. As the passengers climbed aboard, they were forced to pass this obnoxious little girl who was fond of boasting, "My dad's the driver." Notwithstanding that these days I can't stomach the circus, that is a fond memory.

Most Sunday mornings Dad went to Petticoat Lane, a street market that dates from the 17th century and continues to operate today. Only now, it's called Middlesex Street. He always brought something home for me—a doll or a dress or a book—and my mother was often less than pleased with his choices.

One Sunday, there was a pretty yellow dress with a silky fringed bib that frayed and made a bit of a mess. I felt bad when Dad was roundly scolded for his efforts. My mother was so very different from his family, which wasn't either of their faults, but it did create a slowly widening rift between them.

And then she was pregnant.

My first two years of school were at Mary Our Lady of Zion convent. In nursery school (pre-K) I got the measles and was out for two weeks. That meant missing the reading lessons everyone else was getting in my absence. I cried, thinking everyone else had a leg up on me while I was sick. The truth was, I'd taught myself to read when I was three.

When I got back to class, Sister Anne, one of the nice nuns, sat me on her lap and opened the *Meet Dick and Jane* book the class had been using. I can't describe the relief to discover that when I looked at the page, I already knew the words! I could read. And I haven't stopped reading since...

The nuns in my second year were not so gentle. I got my knuckles rapped with a ruler more than once. Probably for talking out of turn. Or touching curtains.

My class was at lunch in the dining room. This was the place where I saw the light about lima beans, which were served with disturbing regularity. I never wanted one to pass my lips, ever again. It was also the place where I got caught touching the lace curtains. Can you blame a kid for being curious about what was going on outside in the playground? For my sins, I was made to stand in the corner for the entire next lunch period. Incorrigible brat that I was, I managed to sneek peeks behind me and was outraged at the loads better food the older girls got than we did in the lower forms.

With my mother expecting a new baby, it was no longer feasible for her to drag me on two buses across London every day to convent school. Ecclesbourne Road Primary School in Islington was within a reasonable walking distance, and I was happy to make the switch.

The school had been built more than 150 years ago—not all that old by British standards. When I visited in the late 90s it was still operating, though it's since been torn down. Sad to think of no more kids joining hands in the playground and circling an unwitting victim, playing "pinch, punch, or join in the ring." Not sad for the victims, though.

Mrs. McMaster was my favorite teacher. Every day, she regaled us with tales of her two cats, Tops and Turvey, and the trouble they got into for doing typical cat stuff like unraveling balls of wool. In those days I was rather like Hermione Granger—a know-it-all—raising my hand and asking for more homework. For all the sums I totted up at home, I should be good at maths. I'm not.

I was keen on British history, especially the civil war—the War of the Roses. We were tasked with drawing the Tudor rose. White on red with five points, it was a symbol of peace and unity after the hostilities between the house of Lancaster (red) and the house of York (white).

We learned about King Canute, the Viking, who sat on his throne at the edge of the sea, supposedly trying to turn back the tide—only he wasn't. He was demonstrating how powerless kings are against God. And let's not forget my heroine, Boadicea, the Celtic warrior queen who led a revolt against Roman rule around A.D. 60. The bronze statue of Boadicea and Her Daughters draws me whenever I'm near Westminster Bridge in London.

But I digress...

Chapter 26

Baby makes four

E arly one morning in 1956 Dad woke me while it was still dark. It was time for the new baby to join the family. As my mother went off to the maternity hospital, I put in my request for a sister. No promises were made.

They didn't bring me the sister I had asked for, but I did get a gorgeously peach-colored baby brother. The coloring was from jaundice. Richard Simon Peter—now just Rick—joined us when I was nearly seven. Another seven years passed before I did get my sister, and unfortunately, the circumstances were less than joyful when I did.

Being a big sister had its ups and downs. Richard didn't always cooperate when I wanted him to be my dolly, and he grew to be as pestiferous as most little brothers are, stealing my diary when I was a young teen and sharing it with my boyfriends, embarrassing me in any number of ways.

With so many years between us it was a long time before we became close. I have to admit, though, he more than redeemed himself in adulthood by providing my kids and me a place to live when we most needed it.

Staying at my grandparents' home was always a treat for me. Nanny had been a concert pianist when she was young, and later taught piano. I was constantly on at her to give me lessons on the baby grand in her sitting room. There's a special place in my heart for that room with its sculpted green sofa and armchair. Nobody made me stand in the corner if I touched those curtains (everybody had lace curtains in those days). Dead certain that gnomes and fairies were hiding in the fluffy black hearth rug, I spent a fair amount of time in front of the fireplace looking for them.

With all my cousins living in other countries, and Richard being too small, at Christmas I was the one who was called on to decorate the tree. I would hang the plastic icicles and tinsel with abandon, breaking my share of glass ornaments as I climbed to place the star at the top. There were candle holders that clipped onto the branches and held actual candles—we're lucky I didn't burn the house down.

It was our family tradition for Nanny to bake an English Christmas fruitcake. She'd let me place the tiny Santa and his sleigh on the thick white sugar icing that covered a layer of marzipan, looking like freshly fallen snow.

After the roast beef and roast potatoes with Yorkshire pudding and brussels sprouts, or lamb with mint sauce, there was trifle made with ladyfingers and English custard, which is quite different from American custard. The adults got brandy in their serving, but Nanny made sure I got the green glass bowl with a sixpence hiding in the cake.

Grandad, who was a professional singer earlier in his life, led us in carols as we gathered around the piano and Nanny played. Aunty Molly had moved to America with Uncle Bob and started their family in Indianapolis. The box of Christmas presents that came from her in the mail served as a tangible symbol of her presence.

Grandad, it turns out, was a WWI war hero. Imagine that. Alfred G. Ahrens, who used to take me with him on long walks, forever reminding me to pick up my feet and stop scuffing my shoes, a war hero!

Joy, one of several cousins I had the pleasure of meeting through Ancestry. com, kindly gave me a mini replica of the medal Grandad received for bravery, along with a small article about him.

"For conspicuous gallantry and devotion to duty. At Vault Vrau-court on the 2nd September 1918, when all his company officers and senior NCOs had been either killed or wounded he led the men forward, and at the point of the bayonet captured three enemy field guns which were defended with stubbornness. His gallantry and disregard of danger when facing heavy odds were a very fine example to his men."

He'd been only twenty-five years old. Like so many veterans, I don't think he ever spoke of what he had experienced; what he had done. Grandad! Who would have guessed?

Many older English houses were given names as well as numbers. Until I read that article, I never knew why my grandparents' home in Worcester Park, Surrey, was named Vraucourt.

Chapter 27

We're moving to America

Richard was a few months old when a knock at the door brought a pair of Jehovah's Witnesses preaching their message of the kingdom. Instead of slamming the door in their faces, my mother invited the ladies inside.

"I will study the Bible with you," she promised, "if you can convince my Jewish husband that Jesus is our Savior."

On a follow up visit, one of the ladies, Winnie Grimes, brought her husband, Roy. He and my dad hit it off and the Bible study began. Wanting to please his wife, Dad cooperated and took the preaching on board. Whether he actually believed what he was being taught is iffy. My guess is, not being religious, he probably didn't care one way or the other. More likely, he went along with it because of plans that were afoot for a huge international convention of Jehovah's Witnesses. It was set to take place in the summer of 1958 in New York City.

Perhaps enticed by the old rumor about America that "the streets are paved with gold," Dad started saving up to make the trip. The salary he made driving a lorry for Bovril (a company that produces a strictly British beef paste that's made into a hot drink) wasn't going to cover such an expensive junket. I'm embarrassed to confess, he started skimming some of the product to sell on the black market.

Over the months, he managed to accumulate two hundred quid—the equivalent of more than two thousand dollars in today's money. One dark night as he left the loading dock, the rain was coming down hard. With the cash in his pocket, Dad covered his bald head with his jacket and dashed to his car. When he got home, the money was gone.

Had the roll of bills fallen out when he put the jacket over his head? Had someone stolen it? He never knew the answer; only that he had to start from scratch.

Possibly a worse punishment than losing the money was having to listen to my mother smugly quote Proverbs 10:2 that ill-gotten gains get you nowhere, and adding for good measure, "Jehovah didn't want you using that dirty money to get to the convention."

Pete Taylor was nothing if not resourceful, and somehow, he made his way to that convention in New York.

Nearly a quarter million people assembled at Yankee Stadium and overflowed to the Polo Grounds—the largest crowd in the city's history. Officially, he went for the convention, but I harbor doubts that he attended many of the Bible lectures during the eight-day event.

Along with more than seven thousand other acolytes, Dad crossed the Bronx on one of the buses the JW Organization had chartered to Orchard Beach, and waded out into the Atlantic Ocean. He fulfilled his promise to my mother that he would get baptized—there was a newspaper photo with him in it—you couldn't miss him. It took two strong men to dip my weighty father backwards under the water and back up again.

He returned home with dollar signs in his eyes and a set of ballerina and grand piano scatter pins for me. "We're moving to America," he proclaimed, and straight away started making plans.

Chapter 28

You'd better get over here

Uncle Bob was an American serviceman who had been stationed in England when he met my mother's sister. He and Aunty Molly agreed to sponsor my dad, and before we knew it, we were seeing Dad off to live with them in Indianapolis until he could send for the rest of us.

My mother and Richard and I packed up our stuff. To my chagrin, I had to give away virtually all of my many dolls and books before we went to stay with Nanny and Grandad until it was time for us to join Dad.

It was midyear when I started my new school in Thorpe Bay, Essex. At nine and shy, I was out of place even before the teacher handed me a former student's half-filled notebook to use. My classmates were not welcoming, and I can't remember making any friends there. On the school bus, one of the boys teased me about my furry white mittens. My smartass retort landed me in hot water: "I don't care what you think, I'm going to live in America. So there." I fell short of sticking out my tongue at him, but I should have.

We'd been in Thorpe Bay for about nine months when Aunty Molly wrote to her sister that she'd better get us over to the States. Molly had a suspicion that my father was having an affair. As Richard was the makeup baby for an earlier indiscretion of my mother's, I suppose Dad might have thought turnabout was fair play.

Borrowing money from grandad, Mum made reservations on a BOAC turbo prop plane, and prepared to bundle us off across the world. Our passport photos made Richard and me look like little Russian refugees.

Mum's Islington JW friends gave us a going away party, at which someone was clever enough to give me my first glass of sherry. Big surprise, I got tipsy and blabbed all the family secrets. Amazing what a laughing audience will bring out in the child of a stage comedian.

The awful ache of waving goodbye to my grandparents at Heathrow Airport clung like a bad cold. Nanny in her best hat; Granddad in his tweed jacket. It must have been hard for them, too, seeing their older daughter and two grandchildren off to America, following their youngest. Uncle Roy's family lived in Kuwait. Only Uncle John was still in England, and he never had children, so after we left, no more grandkids to dote on.

That was the last time we saw Grandad. He died three years later at seventy, a heavy smoker. Heart failure and emphysema got him.

$$\int$$

My first airplane flight and it's a transatlantic one on a prop plane. Eighteen hours with three stops along the way. It's a good bet that's where my fear of air travel started.

First stop Glasgow, Scotland, then Keflavik, Iceland. Somewhere between Iceland and Winnipeg, Canada, I discovered airsickness. It wasn't much different from car sickness, with which I was already fully acquainted, and just as unpleasant. The plane was full and I was separated from Mum and Richard by the aisle, so it was the other passengers in my row who got the pleasure of watching me fill the sick bag. A lot. By the time we reached our final destination, I was ready to be done with airplanes.

In Chicago, Dad met us at the gate —you could do that in 1960. He'd brought me a doll to replace the ones I'd had to leave behind. Sally was three feet tall and wore a silvery blue evening gown, a 'fur' wrap, and high-heeled sandals. Frankly, I didn't much care for her because, molded in one piece as she was, her arms and legs couldn't move. But I was thrilled to see my daddy after such a long absence, and was not about to complain about the doll. I'd had my tenth birthday while Dad was in America, and Richard had turned three.

Before driving to Indy the next day to stay with Molly and Bob for a few weeks, we spent the night at the La Salle Hotel. Richard and I were put to bed in a room adjoining our parents'. After being apart for about a year, they were undoubtedly looking forward to some private time to...well, catch up.

In the middle of the night, I woke up out in the hallway in my nightie, not knowing where I was and frightened to bits. I knocked softly on what I thought was our parents' door, but no one answered. I stood out there shivering, sure that I was doomed to stay there all night.

Amazingly, I eventually found my way back to our room and the self-locking door was ajar. Was a guardian angel or spirit guide protecting me? I'd like to think so.

Welcome to America.

Chapter 29

Hollywood, here we come

And go...

Indianapolis: the ups and downs of two families sharing space meant for one. Two three-year-olds, Richard and our cousin Susan, crayoning on the bedroom wall. Richard biting Susan's arm.

Susan, as you might guess, screamed her little head off. Aunty Molly, who must have been going spare with four extra people in the house, came running. Seeing the teeth marks on her child's arm, she justifiably did what any young mother would do...(?) She bit Richard's arm and let him see how it felt. He never again bit anyone (not even me), but poor Aunty suffered guilt for years afterwards.

And don't ask why I thought it was a good idea to take a bath with cousin Paul, who was four years younger than me. That did not go over well with the parents.

Happier memories included the *Alvin and the Chipmunks Christmas Album*. After hearing that record over and over and over (I really liked it!), Molly and Bob had to be celebrating before we had even closed the doors on Dad's 1954 royal blue Ford Mainline sedan and pointed it at the West Coast.

Hollywood, here we come!

All I remember of that two-thousand-mile long trip is the empty plains of Texas.

Nearly a week after leaving Indy, we were lost in the Los Angeles freeway system, which could confound even a highly experienced driver like my dad. From his time in Indiana, he was used to driving on the wrong side of the road (I know, j/k), but Indy was nothing like L.A.

It felt like hours as we made big circles, seeing the same exit signs as we got on and back on the 101 freeway. Finally, the right exit! But our touristy troubles were not quite finished.

Streetcar rails still ran down the middle of the road. My mother, close to hysterical at this point, lost her words and started yelling, "Pete! Pete! Mind the tram lumps!" It doesn't sound funny now, but it was side-splitting back then. We teased her about it for years.

Friends of Dad's back home in England had hooked him up with apartment managers they knew in L.A. The managers had a studio apartment available on Westmoreland Drive in Silverlake. The building stood in the shadow of the Yellow Pages offices, whose surface was decorated with an immense 3-D phonebook.

The fairytale castle facade of the apartment building was nothing if not misleading. Our apartment was on the first floor of the three-story building, at the rear end of a long, dark hallway. The back door opened onto an alley.

Our parents and Richard slept in the living room on a Murphy bed, which pulled down from a closet in the living room. I slept on a rollaway in the walk-in clothes closet.

I started fifth grade in mid-April. Not fitting in was getting to be a habit. Just as in Thorpe Bay, my classmates were already acquainted with each other and not interested in making new friends. Even worse, they made fun of my funny English accent, and my lunches. So, when my mother gave me a little bag of raisins and dates with my sugar sandwich and the kids said, "Ewwww, what are you *eating?*" I came back with, "Flies and roaches." Clever, eh? Not really, but seeing their smug faces turn horror-struck made me feel superior for a minute or two.

Adding insult to injury, my teacher, Mr. Sturm, who was otherwise nice, insisted I change my handwriting style to the Palmer method taught in the U.S. I knew very well how to write. But the British copybook letter designs I had learned and used for years were different and not acceptable.

Being forced to practice writing pages and pages of Palmer was the pits and I resented it. But what's a powerless little kid gonna do? As a handwriting analyst, I know now that being forced to make this unnecessary change was a subliminal message that I wasn't good enough, and contributed to the poor self-image that was rapidly developing.

Our parents found jobs and Richard was enrolled in daycare. Accustomed to being a latchkey kid from when my mother worked in London, I became one again when summer vacation arrived. Left to my own devices, I hung out with the neighborhood kids. We collected empty glass Seven-Up and RC Cola bottles in a grocery cart and redeemed them for cash or more soda at the supermarket.

Other pastimes the little hooligans engaged in were not so innocuous. Seeing them shoplift candy was a bridge too far for me. Scared that they would get caught and I would be blamed along with them, I started waiting outside the store until they had done their dirty deeds.

They took me to meet an old man who they said was their friend. He lived in an Airstream trailer on an overgrown lot. His thing was trading chocolate Malt Balls candy for kisses on the cheek. Might have been entirely innocent—just some old guy who liked little kids. Nah; something definitely felt off about that.

But far, far worse was Jack Roush.

Chapter 30

Bye-bye innocence

Forty years old and single, Jack Roush was a friend of the apartment managers who we met when my family socialized at their place. Whoever thought it was a good idea for this guy to be allowed to drive a ten-year-old girl around town in his Chevy Impala convertible was a little too trusting. Or downright stupid.

At first, it was more fun than redeeming soda bottles and avoiding the Malt Balls kissing guy. Jack would buy me an ice cream cone and drive me around town. I thought he was really nice. And then, one afternoon, the manager sent me up to his third-floor studio apartment to deliver the mail.

I knocked at his door and he called for me to come in. He was lying in bed in his underwear and told me to bring the mail over to him. When I got close, he grabbed hold of my arm and pulled me on top of him. I had no clue what to do. He was an adult; he had all the power. So, I made like a statue and froze.

Even now, I don't like to think about the details. It could have been worse, but it was plenty bad enough. An hour later when he finally let me go, he said something I remember all too vividly: "If you tell anyone, I'll throw you out the window."

I hightailed it down the stairs to our apartment as fast as I could get my legs to run, and locked myself in the bathroom. If I look hard enough into the past, I can see that curly-haired, formerly innocent child staring at the mirror and spitting into the sink, desperately rubbing at her lips. My mother was due home from work in an hour. If she asked why the edges of my lips were blue, I couldn't very well say, "Because your friend Jack sucked on them for a long time."

There was no question of me telling my parents what had happened, and not because of the threat to throw me out of a third-floor window, though that was a hideous threat to make to a little kid. There was something even more compelling.

When my dad was fourteen, his mother died, and I was familiar with the family lore. Blaming her death on the doctor's delay in coming to the house, young Issy threw the doctor down the stairs. I was desperately afraid that if I told Dad what had happened to me, he would kill the molester and go to prison, and it would be my fault.

Thinking about it now, I am reminded of the police delay in responding to Jennifer's 911 call, and my fear for my sons when Jennifer was killed. History does repeat itself in various unpleasant ways.

For the remainder of the summer, I hid out in the apartment, huddled next to the radio, the volume turned as low as possible and still be able to hear the music. The molester knocked at the door several times, softly calling my name. There was no way I was going to let on that I was in the kitchen, shivering in fear.

Three years later, long after we moved away from that joyless place in Silverlake, my mother mentioned that she'd heard their old pal Jack Roush had died due to complications of diabetes. An image popped into my head of the hypodermic needle I had noticed on a lace runner on top of his dresser. It was safe now to tell her what had happened. There was little reaction.

I shed no tears on his passing, but there is no schadenfreude from me. I have no doubt that once he got to the Other Side, he was required to pay for what he did.

An aside: someone named 'Jack' has come through in a couple of mediumship sessions. I assumed it was my mother's cousin of the same name. But it suddenly occurs to me to wonder if it was the molester, wanting to apologize. If it is, I'm not highly evolved enough to want to hear it.

Chapter 31

Anaheim is not just Disneyland

Dad found a job in Anaheim, famed for being the home of the original Disneyland, and we moved again. These days, Disneyland now bears the much fancier name, 'Disneyland Resort,' and charges much fancier prices. Back then, it wasn't 'all that.'

Not surprisingly, Anaheim Boulevard and Lincoln Avenue look entirely different now than they did in 1961. Downtown meant the SQR department store (too pricey for us to shop there), and the Fox Theater, where we could see *The Parent Trap* for sixty-five cents. Martinet Hardware. Mode O'Day. The drugstore on the corner where we used to stop for hot chocolate on the way to Anaheim High School. Oh, and the record shop that also sold toys—that's where I spent my allowance on many a Barbie and Ken and their wardrobe.

Our introduction to the city was slightly less than red-carpet. My mother had contacted the local Jehovah's Witness Kingdom Hall to say we were moving there and to ask about housing. The family of an elderly couple who had gone into a care home offered the use of their house until we found something suitable.

Apparently, nobody had been there in a while to check it out. We arrived after dark. While Dad was getting our suitcases from the car, Richard and I followed Mom to the back door. She stepped inside and flipped on the light switch.

And started screaming.

Seconds later, we were screaming, too. You might have thought it was a dead body that produced the hysterics but it wasn't. The walls and floor were alive with big brown cockroaches scurrying for cover in the light. Dozens of them, probably more. And no wonder—the fridge and cabinets were crammed with rotten food and jam jars thick with mold.

I don't know what we did once we had all calmed down. A motel, I expect, until Dad started his job as manager of The Colonial Shops.

He had never sold furniture before, let alone Early American furniture. But with his generally sunny personality, cleverness, and showbiz chops—the British accent didn't hurt, either—he succeeding in persuading customers to purchase distressed maple tables and chairs, and sofas and lamps to go with them. He had retained his comedic talent from the stage and you could count on him to produce a corny joke for any occasion. He was good at making people laugh.

He handed out business cards with a head shot—his chubby, smiling face, in a trilby hat, and the words: *"Pete Taylor, weightily yours."*

Following the cockroach contretemps, we found a one-bedroom furnished apartment above Pete the Barber. Once more, my bedroom was the walk-in closet. Thanks to Mrs. Gosling, my early bad babysitter, I was accustomed to being in one.

The apartment was too small for four of us. What followed was several shuffles around a neighborhood where all the streets had girl's names: Mavis Avenue, close to the railroad tracks, where the 4:00 a.m. train whistle was an annoying wake-up call. Pauline Street, where my birthday party was attended by one child—that was before my mother became rabid as a JW and she'd apparently forgotten that they don't celebrate birthdays. Finally, a two-bedroom house on Sabina Street. At last, an actual bedroom of my own.

Sixth grade at George Washington Elementary was a repeat of the teasing (better known today as bullying) I had experienced in L.A over my accent. Plus, after living my first ten years in foggy London, the bright California sun had me squinting. So, I was called "wrinkle nose" (that was you, Lee Stowe). Still, I made friends at GWE, and aside from missing Nanny and Grandad and the familiarity of home, I was happy enough.

$$\text{\large ⟨}$$

For a JW kid the start of each school day was torture. Believing they owe allegiance to God alone, JWs opt to not salute the flag. Everyone else put their hands over their hearts and recited the pledge. I suppose I should count myself lucky that, in addition to "I belong to a weird religious cult," my ready-made excuse was, "I can't pledge allegiance to another country; I'm from England." Not that it stopped people from giving me the side eye.

My classmates handed out Valentine's Day cards and celebrated Thanksgiving, Christmas, political holidays; we JWs had to sit out those events, pretending we didn't care about our self-exclusion.

Worst of all was when the *Star-Spangled Banner* was played. Word came down from the governing body via the *Watchtower* magazine ('God's organ'): if you are already standing at an event where the national anthem begins to play and everyone else in the venue stands up, you may remain standing. If you are seated, however, you must remain seated." Trust me when I say, I always tried to plan in advance to be on my feet when I heard the opening strains, *"O say can you see..."*

We attended three religious meetings a week: an hour-long Bible study on Tuesday nights; the two-hour Ministry School on Thursday, and two more hours on Sunday, a sermon and the *Watchtower* study—a Q&A session for which you are expected to study in advance and have your hand up with the answers to questions printed in the magazine.

In addition, most weekends we had to get up early to knock on doors for an hour or two, annoying people in their homes. Can't say I enjoyed doing that, but it was all I had known for a very long time and it was just part of life. Like brushing your teeth and combing your hair. A necessary evil.

After the door-to-door field service and Sunday meeting, several families, including mine, would meet up at Helen Grace's ice cream shop. Their banana split made up for a lot.

Chapter 32

We're going home

Seventh grade at Fremont Junior High across town, I was feeling very grown up, learning to sew and cook in Mrs. Palmieri's Home Ec class. First project, an apron, then pink babydoll pajamas. The cinnamon toast was the best.

Dad was doing well in sales. Over the next two years he worked, variously, at White Front, Zody's, and Gemco membership department stores (kind of like Costco). We moved into a three-bedroom house where Richard and I had our own rooms. The orange tree in the backyard was made for climbing and nestling in the branches, where I read a ton of mystery novels.

With Dad earning enough money to carry the household, my mother no longer had to work outside the home. That didn't mean she became a stay-at-home mom, however. All that free time gave her plenty of opportunities to engage in Jehovah's Witnessing, and she was preaching 'the good news of the kingdom' more than ever.

Oddly, despite all her years of performing in front of audiences, and despite being able to go door-to-door, preaching to total strangers, my mother was pathologically shy. Or maybe it wasn't all that strange. Her mother, a pianist on the concert stage until she became a victim of the 'casting couch,' was the same. My musically talented Nanny had been invited to perform a concert at the great Royal Albert Hall (like Carnegie)—a high honor. Until the requirements imposed upon her acceptance became clear. She declined.

Much later, my mother forced herself to overcome her shyness. But at that time, when Dad brought friends over to the house to meet her, she would run and hide in their bedroom, refusing to come out as long as they were there. As gregarious as my dad was, I can imagine how uncomfortable and embarrassing it must have been.

We started seeing less of him. Being a young teenager wrapped up in my friends and schoolwork and witnessing and other activities, I didn't pay much attention to Dad's increasing absences. He often came home well after Richard and I were asleep, and we were off to school before he woke up in the morning. I assumed he was working late at night. We were soon to learn that was not the case.

In the summer of 1963, two-and-a-half years after our arrival in America, Dad surprised us all with an announcement: "We're moving back to England."

Without consulting my mother, he had decided that she wasn't happy in the US. She needed to be back home, near her mother, he said. Never mind that she didn't *want* to move back. She had established herself in the Anaheim congregation and made close friends there. And, more importantly, she and her mother didn't get along because of her religion.

When we had lived with Nanny in Thorpe Bay, they fought constantly, and sometimes used me as a pawn. Good little JW-trained robot that I was, I would parrot Bible verses I had learned that appeared to refute some of Nanny's deeply-held beliefs. One thing Jehovah's Witnesses are very good at is teaching their view of the Bible.

Nothing my mother could say could change Dad's mind; we were selling up again and leaving.

As for me, I could not have been more ecstatic. I was going home!

Chapter 33

The guilt trip

We were going on a guilt trip, and I don't mean the kind where you are reminded of past favors, or how much more work someone else has put in. The guilt was my dad's, and it was showcased in the trip back to England: first class tickets on an ocean liner.

It started with a Pan Am flight from Los Angeles to New York in First Class. We were served on china plates—filet mignon with fresh sliced carrots and parsley potatoes—a little different from airplane fare today.

(I say that, but this was the only time I've flown first class, so I could be all wet.)

After boarding a tour bus and getting a cursory look at the Empire State Building and the scenic neighborhoods of New York, like the Bowery, my family trooped up the gangway and were welcomed aboard the SS France.

The France, put into service only a year earlier, was the largest transatlantic ocean liner of its time. I'm sorry to say that the stabilizers on its funnels did nothing to prevent my seasickness the first day out. But after getting a glimpse at the good-looking teenaged French sailors I got my sea legs in a hurry.

Gerard Trebot and his friend Philippe were dangerously adorable in their blue and white striped t-shirts and flat white sailor hats. For a girl about to turn fourteen, chatting me up like they did could have been bad news.

With my short haircut and wearing my mother's chic tight red dress to dinner in the grand salon, I looked years older than I was. The two sailors invited me to meet them after their shift, and I made a plan to sneak out. Sharing a cabin with my little brother probably saved me from myself. Or them. When I heard their knock on our cabin door, I chickened out (maybe it reminded me of Jack the molester knocking at our apartment in L.A.). My guardian angel on duty stepped in, I think.

After the voyage, Gerard and I mailed several postcards back and forth—he signed *"Bon Baiser,"* (good kisses)—but obviously that wasn't going anywhere. Flattering, though.

At the end of a week at sea, the massive ship edged its way into the dock at Southampton. I stood on deck with my face turned to the morning mist and felt kissed: a welcome home.

The incident with Jack Roush three years earlier had soured me on America before I had a chance to get acquainted with our then-new country. My wounded child's heart needed something to blame, and the US was it. Being back in England meant safety and security. Or so I thought.

Grandad had died six months earlier, and Nanny had moved to a house in Chessington, Surrey with her younger son, my Uncle John. Almost as soon as Dad carried our suitcases into the house, he said he had a job interview in the north and would return in a couple of days. We said goodbye to him.

He didn't come back.

One early morning two days after he left I heard the post come through the letterbox. Recognizing my dad's handwriting on one of the envelopes, I ran it upstairs to my mother, who was still in bed. As I was leaving the room her anguished cry stopped me.

Spinning around, I saw a piece of paper clutched in her hand, the envelope on the floor. Unnerved by her wailing, I took the paper from her and read the seventeen words that broke my family:

"By the time you read this I will be on my way back to the United States."

He hadn't even bothered to find something nice to write it on. The message was penned on a sheet that had been torn in half. He had included a fifty pound note (equivalent of around $1000 today). Not fully comprehending what it meant, I went and sat on the stairs, shed a few tears, then went about my day.

After that, just as I used to do on the coach he drove to the circus, where I proudly told the passengers, "My dad's the driver," I began to overshare to anyone who would listen: "My dad just left us."

My mother, who had been willfully blind, was utterly unprepared to be left on her own with two children. All those nights her husband came home in the wee hours, long after the store he worked in had closed for the night, how could she have not known that something was going on? To be fair, she'd had a suspicion about a woman in the accounting department where Dad worked, but she'd let him put her off with excuses: "Roslyn? She's nothing to worry about. I felt sorry for her, took her to lunch."

Mum broke the news to seven-year-old Richard. "My daddy wouldn't leave me," he said, ripping a piece out of my heart.

But his daddy did and Richard never fully got over it. Dad had left all three of us, and what he wrote about being on his way back to the US was a lie. He was actually gallivanting around Europe with his pregnant girlfriend—Roslyn from Accounting. I'm pretty sure he must have been miserable most of the time. Or maybe that's just wishful thinking.

My mother told me she was considering throwing herself in front of a train. That's a lot to dump on fourteen-year-old shoulders. Lucky for my little brother and me, something stopped her. I'm guessing she had a guardian angel, too. Or borrowed one of ours.

Roslyn was divorced from a man with mental problems. Like my father, she was obese and didn't have a lot to commend her in the looks department. Richard and I joked that she had a wart on the end of her nose like a witch. For Dad, the big attraction was, she was more like his family—Jewish. It wasn't about religion—neither of them was devout. It was cultural, a feeling of familiarity. And she wasn't the type to hide in the bedroom when Dad brought friends home like my mother did, and I expect that counted for a lot. Months later, back in the US, he had the nerve to complain to me, "I don't know why you don't like her."

For me, familiarity bred contempt. *Like* her? This woman who threatened to tell me horrible stories about my mother? This woman who had no problem in tearing my family apart for her own selfish aims? Upon learning she was pregnant she had threatened my father: get a divorce and marry her or she would sic her brothers on him. I'm not sure what she thought her brothers were going to do. As far as I know, they were not mafioso; they owned a deli in Brooklyn. I suppose they could have beat him with a kosher salami.

I could write a lengthy chapter about that woman's evil deeds, of which there were many—some shocking—but that's not the point of this story.

As the married father of two, my dad was the one who deserved the greater blame. But let's face it, both parties to an illicit affair are responsible for the fallout. My mother played her role, too. But she didn't deserve what she got. Neither did we.

Chapter 34

Finally, I fit

My father may have deserted his family, but Richard and I still had to attend school. At Chessington Girls School, we wore a uniform of grey pleated skirt and white shirt with a royal blue tie. My classmates loved my American accent as much as the US kids had taunted me for my British one. At last, I fit in. Apart from that thing about my family splitting up, I was reveling in life in England.

The Royal Variety Performance on TV November 4th, 1963 was my introduction to the Beatles and I became an instant Beatlemaniac. The room I shared with my mother was soon papered in Beatles pictures cut from teen magazines. From waking to sleeping, that was all I talked about—a distraction from the glut of painful emotions I was actively working to suppress.

The first story I ever wrote was *To Wed A Beatle*, in which I married Ringo, the underdog. Looking it over sixty years later, I'm pleased to say (in all modesty?) it wasn't badly written.

My very cool Uncle John, who was a bit of a playboy, was dating the actress, Honor Blackman (James Bond's Pussy Galore). In the vernacular of the times, he was *smashing*. He gave me a birthday card with a cartoon 'mop top' on the front. Inside, it said, "that's all she wrote." I didn't know what that meant, but if it had a Beatles reference, I was happy.

One day, I arrived home from school to an empty, silent house. Until then, every day we lived with her, Nanny had been there, making sure tea was ready when I banged through the door.

Teatime in our part of England was akin to supper in the US ('dinner' was lunch). It meant sandwiches or baked beans on toast or Welsh rarebit or homemade fish and chips—that sort of thing. And cake. Most days I could expect to see a Battenburg or a Victoria sponge on the dining room table. Or butterfly cakes Nanny had made, or scones (no wonder I am cursed with a sweet tooth). But that afternoon, for the first time, I was home alone. And it felt as though I was not.

It was an eerie sensation—a distinct feeling of an unseen presence; of being watched by—I don't know what spirit was there with me that day—Grandad? All I know is, someone, or something, was in the house with me. I could feel it, but I couldn't see it, and thanks to my Jehovah's Witness upbringing I was scared spitless.

JW is a fear-based religion and I absorbed a *lot* of that emotion through the pages of *The Watchtower* magazine. I had been taught to fear the spirit world, and that I needed to protect myself from the Devil and his demons—evil spirits who wanted to harm me. I had no clue why any spirit would want to harm me or anyone else, but that alarming message was hammered into my naive mind as ceaselessly as another one they disseminated: I should expect to be persecuted and thrown into prison for my faith someday.

So, that afternoon, trying to mentally barricade myself against 'the demons,' I sat alone in the kitchen, shaking, longing for someone to come home and fill the house with the sounds of their human presence. At last, when they did, I heaved a gusty sigh of relief and kept the eerie sensation to myself. If I'd told her about it, my mother would have freaked and moved us out of the house on the spot.

I wish I had told Nanny, though. She would have understood and probably would have said something helpful—something that might have saved me from years of fear—something that would have started me on my spiritual path a whole lot sooner.

Chapter 35

Back to the future

My mother, convinced that the husband who had deserted her might try for a 'quickie Mexican divorce' and get custody of us kids, was determined to bring us back to the US and try for a reconciliation. Her reasoning was specious at best. With us in England, and being British citizens, I can't imagine he could have worked that out if he'd tried. Nor can I imagine Roslyn—four years younger than my mother and expecting her first baby—agreeing to take on her lover's seven- and fourteen-year-old kids.

My pleas to stay in England fell on deaf ears. Nanny was happy to have me, but as a staunch member of the Church of England, she deplored the JW teachings my mother preached at her, and vice-versa, so if I were to stay behind, there was no guarantee that I would attend the three weekly meetings at the Kingdom Hall and go in door-to-door service. Who are we kidding? I would have found the first excuse not to go.

So, dragging my heels hard enough to carve ruts in the floor I packed up my stuff and once again said goodbye to my beloved grandmother, my Uncle John, and the home I loved.

❦

Our Pan Am flight landed at LAX on Pearl Harbor Day, 1963. Billie and Shirley Schmitt, parents of my friend Terry and her four siblings, had invited us to stay with them in Anaheim until we could get settled. Again.

The day after our arrival, a lightning strike crashed Pan Am's Flight 214 over Maryland, killing all 81 passengers. I have successfully completed many dozens of flights since then, but I white-knuckled every one of them. I suppose that the accident being the same airline we'd flown, so close to our arrival in the US got tangled up in my subconscious.

Billie Schmitt was the "congregation servant" (i.e., chief JW elder), and my mother had a crush on him. After we moved into an apartment on Chartres Street she made a habit of dumping on him about her rebellious daughter, yours truly. I knew this because at school one day, Terry informed me that her dad had gathered his five kids together and used me as a bad example not to follow. He shared the latest of my sins that my mother had spilled the beans about—probably back-talking her, which was as bad as I got. And she wondered why I didn't confide in her.

My school friends welcomed me back to Fremont Junior High. Thanks to the Beatles' appearance on the Ed Sullivan Show, I was now a minor celebrity. I had brought their first two albums back with me, along with several pair of fishnet stockings, which were soon to be all the rage.

This time, the other kids thought my accent was groovy because I sounded like the Beatles. Well, not really—they were from Liverpool and I was from London. That's the difference between a New York accent and an Alabama one, but I was from England like the "Fab Four," and that's what counted.

Each day, my friends would look for me, eager to read the next chapter in my latest Beatles story. I was pounding them out on the ancient Remington typewriter Dad had bought me, and binding the onionskin sheets in a folder for them to check out like a library book. The list of those friends' signatures is on the first page.

Dad got visitation rights on Monday nights, which usually meant a walk around the store where he worked, looking for bargains, and maybe a meal in the cafeteria or a neighborhood diner.

After many a loud argument with my mother, he gained permission to take us to the condo he shared with Roslyn.

I was less than thrilled to meet my father's paramour. One thing my dad appreciated about Roslyn was her cooking. My memory of our first visit was the pungent aroma of gefilte fish as we walked in the door (none for me, thanks). I expect I pulled a face, but agreed to try the borscht, and a beef roast. Everything had a strong taste of garlic, which was new to me. My mother wouldn't be found in the same room with it. Or mayonnaise. Or salad dressing. You get the idea. Picky.

We hadn't been back in the US for very long when Roslyn phoned my mother and wanted to "talk about the situation over lunch."

We didn't have a car. Our red Plymouth Valiant had been sold before our return to England. Or so we thought. Before we were able to get a piano and my mother started teaching, to eke out a living, she was walking miles to clean other people's houses. When Roslyn showed up *in our Valiant* to pick her up, it was like a punch in the face.

Using stunningly bad judgment (in my opinion), my mother actually went to lunch as a passenger in what had been her car. Considering the shamelessness it took to be so openly and aggressively unkind, it should not have been a surprise that Roslyn made an outrageous suggestion.

"Pete and I know you're short of money," she said, pretending she gave a crap. "So, we thought you could babysit for us when our baby is born."

Clinging to some last shred of dignity, my mother declined. And yet, weirdly, she continued to harbor hopes of a reconciliation. When Dad left us she didn't know how to balance a checkbook, or pump gas—she was good at playing the damsel in distress card, prevailing on some random guy at the gas station to do it for her. So, maybe there was a method to her madness. She needed someone to take charge.

On the night of May 31st, 1964, while my parents were together at our apartment, making plans to get back together, Roslyn went into labor. The next day, I had the (half) sister I had requested seven years earlier, Sara Beth.

My father decided to stay with his new family and leave the old one behind. "Roslyn isn't as strong as you are," he informed his wife, "She can't make it on her own."

I guess he missed the part about my mother threatening to jump in front of a train not so long ago.

The divorce became final and he married Roslyn. From then on, virtually everything he did was to benefit her and their baby.

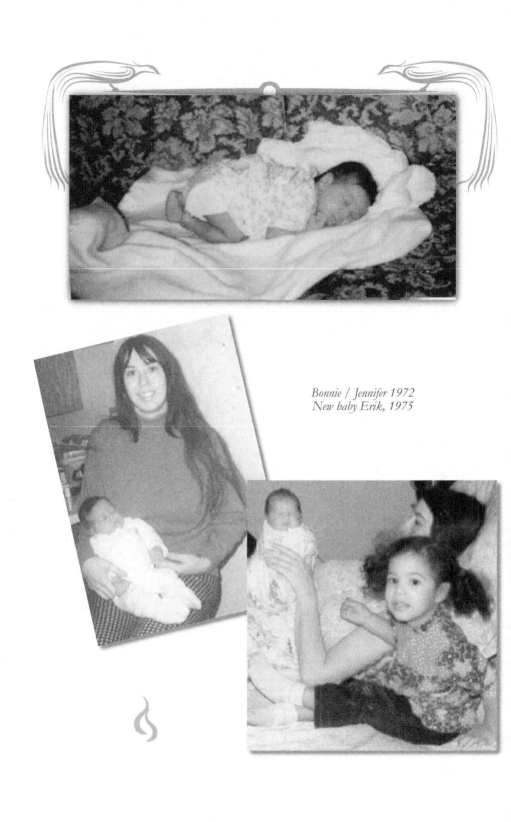

Bonnie / Jennifer 1972
New baby Erik, 1975

Bonnie / Jennifer 1972
The Lowe kids and mom, circa late 1997 or so
Below: Jennifer and baby Charlie

Sheila holding Ben, with Erik 1978

Above: Erik Doug, Ben 2001
Below left: Ben, right: Erik

*Sheila with Jennifer and at
second wedding to Bill, 1999*

Below right: Jen and Scott, 1998

Jennifer and Tom, 1999

"Vicky King: in pantomime - first girl in front. Aunty Molly 7ᵗʰ girl back in hat

Pete "Weightily Yours" Taylor

Left: Jean Susan
right: Richard/Rick

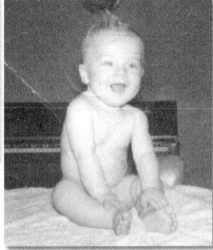

Left: Sheila eating a cornet:
Below: Sara

*Above: Sheila & Bill
at Iseldon House
Left: Pete & Vicky
wedding
Below: Pete & Roslyn*

*Above, family Christmas
(Sheila behind the piano in the hat)
Left: Grandad the war hero
right: Nanny the concert pianist*

Saying goodbye to Dad who is going to America
Nanny, Sheila, Richard, Mum

Sheila's passport photo
Richard, Dad

Above, apartment on
Westmoreland
Left: Sheila, still innocent

Below right: The Valiant

Top: Ecclesbourne Rd. School

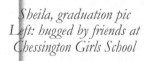

Sheila, graduation pic
Left: hugged by friends at
Chessington Girls School

Top left: Mum, Nanny, Sheila
Top right: Sheila's psychedelic dress
Below left: Ken, Sheila, 1965
Below right: Sheila wedding (deer in headlights)

right: Bill and Sheila first wedding

Left: Bob Joseph with
Sheila and Bill
First wedding reception

Above: Bill and Sheila second wedding

Roger Rubin, Sheila, 2010

Above left: Charlie Cole, Sheila, 1990
Below: Roger Rubin, Felix Klein

Si Cohen, Sheila

Above: James Van Praagh
Right: Sheila, Sonia Rinaldi
Below: with Tina Powers
At AREI Symposium, Scottsdale

*Arnie and image he sent from spirit
through Sonia Rinaldi*

*Bill and image he sent from spirit
through Sonia Rinaldi*

Happy Holidays

Jen and two images she sent from spirit through Sonia Rinaldi

Not very Christmas-y
but I thought it
was cute.
Happy Holidays.
Jennifer

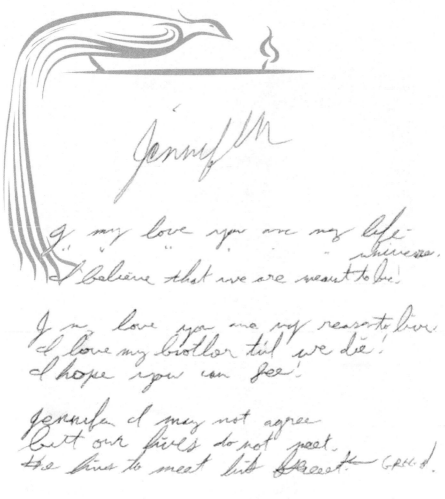

Jennifer

J, my love you are my life.
I believe that we are meant to be!

I'm love you are my reason to live.
I love my brother til we die!
I hope you can see!

Jennifer I may not agree
but our lives do not meet.
the time to meet but greet.

Above, letter from Tom Schnaible
Below: "Sign" sent by Jennifer

Chapter 36
The Hand of Mary Constable

My friend Julie was visiting from the Bay Area. She and I took a walk across town to the Anaheim Public Library, where I was known to spend an inordinate amount of time browsing the shelves for mystery novels. For some reason I cannot now fathom because I certainly knew better, I checked out a book titled *The Hand of Mary Constable* by Paul Gallico.

In my defense, I was intrigued by its black cover and upturned disembodied white hand. It called to me from the library shelf. I couldn't help myself; it sucked me in. Okay, I'll stop. I admit it, I made an error of judgment. At sixteen, errors of judgment are to be expected.

That book was later made into a TV movie of the week, *Daughter of the Mind*, with Ray Milland and Gene Tierney. Billed as a horror-thriller, it tells the story of a renowned scientist who believes that his 10-year-old daughter, who has died of leukemia, is trying to contact him from the dead.

I never got a chance to read it.

That night, after getting up to all the silliness only a couple of teenage girls could get up to; after all the Pepsi had been drunk, all the pizza eaten, and we had giggled ourselves into exhaustion, Julie and I climbed into our jammies and crashed in my room.

It was the middle of the night and we were deep in dreamland when my mother burst in and shook me awake. "What have you brought into the house?" she demanded in a high-pitched voice that scared me. "Did you bring something with the demons attached to it?"

Demons? She was scaring Julie and me out of our wits.

Richard had woken up to find a large, dark, shadowy—*something*—hovering next to his bed. He wasn't afraid of it, just startled. In adulthood he has assured me that whatever, or whoever it was, it didn't feel menacing. But our mom was losing her shit and accusing me of bringing evil spirits into the house.

Uh oh.

There was only one thing I could think of that might possibly account for what my little brother had seen. Figuring I was about to be grounded for the rest of my life, I reached under the bed and slid the library book from its hiding place.

My mother took one horrified glance at that black cover and its white hand. Faster than the proverbial speeding bullet, *The Hand of Mary Constable* flew out the kitchen door and landed in the backyard. It's surprising that my mother would touch it. Or maybe she had me do it and I've forgotten that bit. Either way, I was in big trouble—no phone for a week, and no parties for a month (not that she ever stuck to those punishments).

First thing in the morning, before the library opened, Julie and I made the mile-long trek to return the book into the big outdoor book depository.

I still haven't read that book, but I probably should.

Strangely, it was always my mother who was involved in the supposed "demonic" experiences I heard about. Years after the library book event, when I was married to Ken, and she was living with a JW friend, another event occurred.

For some unknown reason there was a stack of wooden two-by-fours on one of the twin beds in her room. My mother was getting ready to go to sleep when suddenly a loud rapping noise came from the wood. She yelled for her housemate, Nicki, who entered the room and, as the story goes, suddenly went ice cold and 'water' started streaming from her eyes.

The two of them started frantically searching for what might have brought the demons into the house. The only thing my mother could think of was an old Catholic Bible that my husband had bought from a secondhand store and loaned to her.

Paging through it they came across notes someone had handwritten next to passages about the evils of divination and the occult. The notes supposedly said that these practices were good and should be followed.

Now, please suspend disbelief for the next bit. Triangular-shaped pieces cut from some of the pages fell out of the book. Nicki and Mom took them to the stove, but—eye roll here—they wouldn't burn. Like that library book, the Bible went into the backyard until the next day, when they called their friend Paul to come and burn it in the barbecue.

I have several problems with this scenario. First, there were never any 'demonic visitations' while the Bible was at my house. Second, after Paul, a JW minister, died (nothing to do with the 'demonic Bible'), the young child of a friend of mine reported that Paul had regularly held him at gunpoint and forced him to perform sexual acts on him. The explicit magazines and firearm found in Paul's apartment suggested that the boy was telling the truth.

So, these two women were looking to a secret child molester as their savior from a supposed demonic Bible. How does that make sense?

Chapter 37

In the beginning...

"*How did you get started in handwriting analysis?*" That question is asked at virtually every presentation or lecture I've ever given—hundreds of them. The answer can be traced back to 1967.

I was a senior at Anaheim High School when I started seriously dating Ken Lowe. We'd known each other since my return from England, and our families attended the same congregation. With six kids in tow (a seventh was grown and gone), the Lowes invariably showed up late for meetings and didn't hang around long afterwards.

Ken was nearly three years older than me, but we socialized in the same circle, and he and his fraternal twin brother, Karl, played guitar in a band called the Sha-Fe's. I have no idea what a Sha-Fe is, but it was cool to know the band members.

Their mother, Elizabeth Lowe—yes, the very same one who chose the furniture for our apartment—had read a book about handwriting analysis and asked if I would like her to analyze mine. Was I going to say no? Of course not. I jumped at the offer.

Elizabeth was an amateur who went chapter-by-chapter of the book she used, copying out sentences that she believed applied to my handwriting. As I pored over the two-page handwritten analysis she gave me with growing excitement, I felt as though someone finally 'got' me.

Here's a small excerpt of what I read:

"When this writer falls in love, it is not the emotional, spontaneous reaction which might peter out too soon. The affections might not be disclosed in a demonstrative manner, they are more often shown through loyalty and the little everyday acts of kindness and devotion."

I liked that!

"The writer is subject to moods. The intellect and emotions are in conflict. The mind wants to do one thing, the heart another. Caution is in conflict with impulsiveness. Often critical of trifles." She called me 'stormy.'

I didn't like that part as much, and it seemed to contradict the first part. But I had to admit, it was all true. Many years later, it occurred to me that when Elizabeth Lowe analyzed my handwriting, she was checking me out as a potential daughter-in-law.

That analysis instantly hooked me on the topic. I devoured the few books about handwriting analysis on the library shelves. Then, in a grocery checkout line, a rack of tiny Dell booklets caught my eye. One was simply titled *Handwriting Analysis*. I didn't stop to think twice. I bought it and started practicing on my friends.

Jehovah's Witnesses don't celebrate secular holidays, but they do have parties. On many Saturday nights you could find me at one, not just dancing and flirting, of which I did my fair share, but often, I would be sitting on the sofa with a line of teenagers waiting for me to analyze their handwriting. Since I didn't know what I was doing, I copied Ken's mother's method and went through my little booklet page by page, decoding what I thought each handwriting sample meant, and sharing my findings with the writer. For an introvert, it was the perfect way to get my closeness at a distance.

Chapter 38
Moving North

My dad, who was no longer a JW, wanted me to go to law school after graduation. However, the Witnesses' governing body strongly discourages higher education in favor of 'putting the kingdom first.' Living with my mother, it had never occurred to me to go further after graduating high school. It wasn't until my 50s that Bill encouraged me to go back and get my degrees.

After high school rather than heading to college, I packed my suitcase and typewriter, and moved four hundred miles north to the Bay Area to live with Julie and her parents in Redwood City. Taking a bus to the San Mateo Hillsdale Shopping Center I got a job at a children's shop steaming wrinkles out of tiny dresses for $1.75/hour.

The living arrangement didn't work out beyond a few months, and after a bitter argument with my now-former friend, I phoned my mother and said, "Can I come home?" Since she had been less than thrilled for me to be so far away, she was delighted to have me return to the nest.

In 1967, a PSA (Pacific Southwest Airlines) flight from SFO to LAX cost $12. Oh, the struggle, carrying all those bags through the airport—luggage didn't have wheels in those days.

At LAX, I caught the $3 airport bus to the Disneyland Hotel, where my mother picked me up. Back then, we got along like girlfriends, going out to lunch and joking about the alluring desserts in the restaurant's pastry case. "They're never as good as they look," we would chant together as a way to resist temptation. Now, she's 94 and thanks to the JWs, has refused to see me since Jennifer's funeral. In dementia, she told me a few years ago, "I never had children." Okay, then.

For a while I settled back into Southern California life, dating boys from the local congregations, including Ken, mostly in groups, and doing the religion as I had since I was a child—lugging a book bag packed with *Awake* and *Watchtower* magazines from door to door, and giving six-minute presentations in the Ministry School.

Women who joined the Ministry School were not allowed to directly teach the men in the congregation, but they could teach another 'sister.' When assigned to give a talk, you would write out a dialogue—a situation that covered the assigned material—and present it with another 'sister.' I gave my first talk in the Ministry School when I was eleven.

That's one thing I can be grateful that I got from my years as a JW—learning how to do public speaking. It made it possible for me to teach, deliver lectures, and appear in the media—even on national shows—with some degree of aplomb.

I think.

⸎

1967 was the 'Summer of Love,' and despite my falling out with Julie, I longed to be back in the Bay Area.

It was the year of the six-day Arab-Israeli war; Mohamad Ali lost his world heavyweight boxing championship for refusing military service during the Vietnam War. Thurgood Marshall became the first black justice. It was the year of *Sergeant Peppers Lonely Hearts Club Band*, and Twiggy, the anorexic British fashion model, was all the rage in her teeny-tiny miniskirts.

It was also the year of Haight-Ashbury, where the counterculture was born. Not that I planned to join the youth who came from all over the US to frequent the head shops. As a goody-two-shoes Jehovah's Witness I didn't smoke pot or drop acid or sleep around, though I secretly wanted to. The truth is, after all she had been through with my dad, I didn't want to disappoint my mother, who would be (and later was) devastated if I got into trouble with the JW organization.

My only outward homage to the hippie culture was my Beatles haircut, and the psychedelic-colors in the clothes I made myself. I was convinced that in my bell bottom pants and tie-dye granny dresses, I looked totally groovy, man.

An invitation came to move back to Redwood City and share a penthouse. I couldn't say yes fast enough. I told Ken I was leaving, and asked facetiously if he would cry. His response came in a poignant poem:

> *When you have gone*
> *I will not cry,*
> *I'll just die.*
> *I am going to have to kill*
> *What I have built for you.*
> *Is that worse than crying?*

There were only three bedrooms, but the penthouse was immense. My friend Nancy and I shared a room. Evelyn was quite a bit older than us and had a room to herself. Priscilla and Bernard were a couple old enough to be our parents, and acted like it.

Nancy and I were eighteen, our boyfriends in their early twenties. The guys attended the local Kingdom Hall and knew Priscilla and Bernard. Still, if they were visiting beyond the strict ten p.m. curfew imposed on us, Priscilla would come and stand in the doorway to the living room and embarrass us by declaring, "Time to put the cats out," after which, she would escort the guys to the front door.

Priscilla and Bernard went out of town for the weekend, warning, "No boys in the apartment while we're not here." It was okay if we had them over to swim, and naturally, we did. We had a blast, eating around the pool, playing in the water; all fairly innocent.

We said goodnight to Jim and Nick and Jerry, and Nancy and I went up to the penthouse, babbling about the fun we'd had. A few minutes later, a knock came at the door. The guys had forgotten their towels.

They were standing in the foyer, waiting for Nancy to bring the towels out, when Bernard and Priscilla showed up early from their trip.

If the nightly "Time to put the cats out" was humiliating, the scene Priscilla made that night was ego crushing. She and Bernard refused to listen to the innocent explanation, and the boyfriends were thenceforth banned from the penthouse.

Meanwhile, I was corresponding with Ken. Long-distance phone calls were mostly out of the question, and except for emergencies, much too expensive to indulge in. In those days, people still put pen to paper and expressed their thoughts and feelings via the mail. 'Snail mail' was far off in the future.

After a few months in Redwood City, I was on my way home again.

Ken wanted to get married.

Chapter 39

Becoming a handwriting analyst

I continued to read books about handwriting, fascinated and often frustrated by the contradictions that popped up in most of the samples I tried to analyze. The books all had different interpretations of the same features, and "This means X" wasn't always true. I needed to know how to resolve the contradictions so that my analyses made sense.

And yet, it was ten years before I discovered there were courses I could take. By then, I was married to Ken and we had three kids. Ben, the youngest, was only a few months old when I read about Charlie Cole's Handwriting Analysis Workshop Unlimited. Excited, I signed on and dove in headfirst.

As I was first being introduced to handwriting analysis in 1967, Charlie Cole was establishing the American Handwriting Analysis Foundation. I began attending Orange County Chapter meetings, and learned a lot from experienced graphologists ('graphology' is the generic term for the study of handwriting).

I heard about Felix Klein, an Austrian graphologist who had begun studying handwriting at the age of thirteen. After surviving the barbarous concentration camps at Buchenwald and Auschwitz in his late twenties, he had immigrated to New York and set up Manhattan Handwriting Consultants.

In the days I knew him, Felix had the look of a kindly gnome. With his Austrian accent and sweet smile he was a favorite lecturer at seminars and conferences. As he related the story of how his knowledge of graphology had on one occasion made his life a little bit easier in the camps, we hung on every word.

During roll call one morning, Felix found himself singled out by a Nazi guard—something to be avoided at all costs. Trembling in his threadbare boots, he stepped forward as ordered, not knowing whether he was about to be shot, or perhaps taken to the gas chamber. Instead, the guard marched him to the house of the commanding officer, which was more than a little strange.

The C.O. had heard about Felix's skill as a handwriting analyst, and he wanted his own handwriting analyzed. It was during the freezing European winter, and the officer's house was warm. With a secret smile, Felix related to us how he had stretched the analysis process, making it take all day to prepare his report.

When he could delay no more, he shared his findings with the officer, who was impressed with what he heard. The man wanted to know whether Felix recommended that he stay in the military after the war.

"You should not be a soldier," Felix responded, hoping his answer would not anger the C.O. "You should be a farmer."

Far from being angry, the officer told him that before being conscripted into the army he had actually been a farmer, and wanted to return to his former occupation. The analysis was confirmation for him. He then asked Felix what he wanted in return for his work that day.

"A cheese sandwich, please," said the starving graphologist.

"Very well," the officer replied, "a cheese sandwich you shall have."

At the next morning's roll call, Felix was called out of line again. Guards and prisoners were not allowed physical contact, and the guard extended his bayonet. Impaled on the tip of the blade was a bag that contained a cheese sandwich.

On Saturday night when the prisoners were released from work, they had a party. Felix divided the sandwich into small pieces and shared them with everyone in his barracks.

In addition to learning something about his beautiful humanity from this act, what Felix Klein taught me about gestalt graphology opened my eyes to a better way of analyzing handwriting, and explained the contradictions that had troubled me for so long. This was the next major step in a career that has now spanned more than fifty years.

I can't leave this section without at least mentioning Roger Rubin, though I could never fully express the significant role he has played in my life. He was a protege of Felix's who has been there for me since 1985 in oh-so-many ways. Any time I have needed a shoulder to cry on, or a tricky handwriting sample to discuss, or anything else, Roger has always picked up the phone. He has given me dialogue for my character Dr. Zebediah Gold in my Forensic Handwriting series—notably, "put your panties over your heart," and many others.

Meeting Felix and Roger was the next major step in a career that has now spanned more than fifty years.

But trouble was coming.

Chapter 40

Bionetix

Ken got interested in microcomputers. The RadioShack TRS-80 was just coming onto the market, but very few consumers had yet to see the need to purchase a home system. After attending an electronics show my husband came home and said, "I want to buy a computer; let's sell the Pinto."

I was not totally in love with the idea of giving up my car to buy a computer. Once I warmed to the idea, though—some convincing was required—Ken's sister Kathy bought the Pinto from us and we replaced it with a '65 Mustang—five years older but a definite step up.

There were no commercial programs available for the PolyMorphics Systems 8080 bus microcomputer that Ken brought home, and the BASIC programming language had to be loaded from a cassette tape every time you turned it on. A speck of dust on the tape meant starting over, but my husband, a great fan of math, was enthralled.

He was chomping at the bit to learn how to program that orange metal box, and spent many hours working on a math program called Roses. After figuring out how to make two pixels race each other as if they were rudimentary cars at the drags, he proposed that we write a program to analyze handwriting. The name we chose, *Bionetix,* was intended to convey a blending of human and machine.

I composed the many pages of text that he subsequently programmed, with no inkling that they would form the basis, nearly twenty years later, of professional software called *Sheila Lowe's Handwriting Analyzer,* which has been sold around the world since 1997.

We advertised in a magazine: computerized handwriting analysis for $10—a multi-page analysis printed on a daisy wheel printer and snail mailed to the customer.

But the togetherness of collaboration on writing the program notwithstanding, there were cockleburs in the love nest; there always had been.

◌

I had analyzed Ken's handwriting early on, but I didn't know enough to properly understand what it was telling me. Sharing poetry was not enough to make a successful relationship. In some important ways, we were not well suited. Like Tom Schnaible, our daughter's eventual killer, Ken had a strong authoritarian streak. It wasn't entirely his fault—that's what Jehovah's Witnesses encourage in their men.

What I didn't understand early on was, his handwriting showed a suspicious nature; a distrust that rose to the level of paranoia. It manifested in him questioning *everything* I did or said. Being hit with the third degree every day of your life is no way to live.

If I were to analyze Ken's miniscule handwriting for the first time today, I would be better equipped to identify the essential anxiety and defensiveness. I would see that it reflected a constant worry that something might go wrong to the point of turning it into a self-fulfilling prophecy.

And because I was too young and, in the beginning, believed I loved him, I overlooked the negatives that I did see. On the positive side, when it came to providing for his family he was highly responsible. And he was very, very intelligent, as well as an excellent JW elder, even if he didn't apply to himself the principles he taught others so well.

I had a lot to learn. Coming from a broken home and parents who didn't know how to parent, I was floundering. There's no value in hurting my kids by publicly detailing the problems I faced, and my marriage to their father is not the main point of my tale. So, I will relate only one small example of the many silly conflicts that over the course of time built molehills into a mountain.

I freely admit that I've never been much of a Suzy Homemaker. I did what needed to be done, but I'd rather be doing just about anything other than cleaning house. If you love being a homemaker, I applaud you and am not putting you down. It's just not what *I* was good at.

On Tuesdays, I did a general housecleaning. I sewed most of the kids' and my clothes, cooked nutritious meals, and handled the million things it takes to keep a household of five going. Plus, there was the JW door-to-door work and meetings three times a week.

The house might not pass a white glove test, but the beds were made, the bathrooms clean enough, and it was dusted and swept. Usually. I wasn't so good at mopping floors.

My husband frequently complained that the kitchen floor was sticky—three little kids, remember? One July 4th he was home from work and took it upon himself to wash the floor. That's great. Except he washed it three times that day. It may sound like a ridiculous thing to bring up, but it was fraught with a lot of arguing and yelling and threats of violence. Multiply that by a few thousand days like it and sometimes, fear enough for me to sleep locked in the kids' room. It's not good for kids to witness. It's not good for anyone.

The fact that I refused to just 'take it,' and be a submissive wife made the atmosphere between us increasingly unpleasant. Unfortunately for Jehovah's Witnesses, when the situation in a marriage becomes untenable there is no option to separate or divorce. More than once I complained to the body of elders in our congregation about what was happening in our home, but it was like the pre "Me-Too" days. An old boys club who wanted to protect their own. One of them even said to me, "Oh, we all feel like hitting our wives sometimes."

Ken was a JW rock star. I had to bite my tongue when one of the 'sisters' said, with a rapturous expression, "It must be like a spiritual banquet, living with him."

He was an effective counselor when others were having problems of one kind of another. He taught the Bible as few could, and was invited to present at major conventions. On the outside, I was married to an exemplary elder who gave interesting and instructive talks from the podium. On the other hand, my insightful three-year-old daughter, watching one of those talks, asked, "Mommy, why isn't he like that at home?"

Chapter 41

Saturation point

We had been renting a house for several years and were talking about buying a place of our own. Despite Ken's objections, it was clear that I would need to take a part time job and help save for a down payment.

Vivian and Rodney were friends of ours from the Kingdom Hall, and their two boys were very close in age to Erik and Ben. We hired Vivian to babysit and I returned to work at JC Penney's, where, in the early days of our marriage, I had worked on the sales floor. Unlike my dad, I wasn't cut out for sales, and had been raked over the coals by the store manager for not being friendly enough to the customers. This time, they put me in charge of employee scheduling, where I screwed up a lot of people's schedules over my short tenure.

On my first day, I worked a four-hour shift. When I arrived home, Ken greeted me at the door: "I can see you're already getting too independent."

The babysitting didn't work out well, either. Having taken a strong dislike to Vivian, Bonnie poured a bottle of Nair hair remover into her shampoo. She found out in time, but Vivian, who had waist-length hair, was understandably upset. I guess she got over it, though. She and Ken got married the same week our divorce, and hers from Rodney, became final.

Things went downhill fast, and it all came to a head on a drive to Disneyland.

ζ

Disneyland! The kids could hardly contain themselves. They clambered into the 'way back' of our lemon-colored Ford Torino station wagon, which had replaced my Mustang, and were excited to be going to the 'Happiest Place on Earth.'

In 1980, the entry fee got you a 10-coupon ticket book—$9.50 for adults, $4.50 for kids—unlike today, where you have to mortgage your house for a family pass at Mickey D's. The coupons started with crappy A-tickets. They were good for the Main Street Cinema or the tame carousel—stuff nobody cared about. The best ones were E-tickets for rides like the Jungle Cruise or Space Mountain or the Haunted Mansion—not that any good JW would be caught dead at the Haunted Mansion—they might bring home some demons! That's what they were told, anyway.

If this sounds nonsensical, try this: they believe the Smurfs are evil and demonic. There's a tale you can find via Google about a child who is said to have woken up in the night to find the Smurfs had jumped off the curtains in her room and were dancing around, laughing satanically. I swear to God. Not that it happened; that they believe it.

So, E-tickets. If memory serves, only two were included in each coupon book, which meant that when it came to the best rides you had to be selective. We were on the freeway when Ken wanted to decide in advance which E-ticket rides we would go on, and he had some definite ideas about that. Our choices, as usual, diverged. He started screaming how much he hated me.

We're with the kids on the way to Disneyland and he's screaming that he hates me.

That was the moment when I knew, crystal clear, that this was it. Eleven a lot of years of trying to be the good submissive JW wife of an elder who was, let's face it, in some ways abusive. I had reached my saturation point.

As far as I was concerned, my marriage was over.

Chapter 42

It doesn't get better

From the photos we took that day, it looks like the kids had a good time at Disneyland, but it's all hazy to me. My monkey mind was scrambling for answers: how was I going to make my exit with the kids?

Having been raised in the JW cult from the age of seven, I believed what I had been taught—that this religion was, as they call it, 'the truth,' and divorce was a big no-no.

My mother was doing missionary work in Louisiana, and of no help when I would phone to complain about abuse I was experiencing. She wanted me to pray and suck it up because, "Jehovah wants you to be a good wife." My mother-in-law's advice— "Just let it run off you like water off a duck's back" —didn't cut the mustard, either.

In 1981 there were no shelters in Orange County California for women and children in distress. I called social services for help and was told I should be glad I had a station wagon for my kids and me to sleep in if necessary.

With no money of my own and nowhere to go with kids ages 3, 6, and 8, I was wracking my brains as to what to do.

And then I did something stupid. I became insanely smitten by a friend who was separated from his much younger wife. Nothing happened between us while I was still in my marriage, but it accelerated my need to move out.

He was the subject of one of my better poems:

I see your face across the miles
Why can't it be?
I'll take you as you are
Take me

My 'little' brother Richard (22), now called Rick, had married Sandy, a woman he had met while living in the South, and brought her back to Southern California, where they had a baby girl, Ashley. A skilled carpenter, Rick started a waterbed manufacturing business, The Old San Francisco Waterbed Company.

He offered for the kids and me to move in with his family in their two-bedroom duplex. My kids would share one of the bedrooms and I could sleep on the couch. In return, I would babysit Ashley some of the time, and cook some meals. It was an offer I didn't want to refuse.

While Ken was at work, I got out my toolbox and took apart the kids' bunk beds. I loaded them into the station wagon, along with clothes and toys and as many of our personal possessions as I could fit. With a gut-wrenching blend of desperation, gratitude, and a smattering of guilt, I drove away from life as I had known it for more than eleven years.

I returned with a truck for the washer and dryer and my sewing machine. And my typewriter, of course. Living with Rick and Sandy came with its own set of problems, but their kindhearted hospitality saved me.

Some years ago, I took a course called *Writing the Breakout Novel* with Donald Maas, a well-known literary agent. What Donald taught that day boiled down to this: Put your hero in a bad situation, then, make it worse. And then, do something that makes it even worse. In the middle of the story, do something to make it as bad as it can possibly get. And then, make it worse.

If my life had been a novel, this would be the major plot point in Act 2. None of it was easy. In fact, it was frigging hard, hard, hard, and it was about to get harder.

Chapter 43

Shunned

Disfellowshipping: *When a judicial committee decides that a baptized Witness has committed a serious sin and is unrepentant, the person is disfellowshipped.*

For Jehovah's Witnesses, disfellowshipping is a BFD. It means being shunned by *all* Jehovah's Witnesses, including close family members living in the same household.

When I left him, Ken accused me of the 'serious sin' of infidelity. It wasn't true, except maybe in my heart.

Infidelity is one cause for disfellowshipping. Other 'serious sins' that merit such a punishment include smoking cigarettes, drug use, selling lottery tickets or firearms, working in an abortion clinic, church or military base, promoting teachings that are counter to JW teachings. Like that.

According to Google, around 70,000 JWs a year become disfellowshipped. Such an action follows a lengthy 'committee meeting.'

You don't ever want to be called into a committee meeting.

For three hours, I was questioned by a committee of old men—excuse me, elderly elders—in disgusting detail about any sexual activities I might have engaged in with the person I mentioned earlier—the object of my infatuation. It was bloody awful. Humiliating. Demeaning.

"Were you naked?"

"Where did he touch you?"

"Where did you touch him?"

And so on, worse and worse.

The congregation elders, who are always men, are godlike in their power. In the rare case when a woman is called on to offer prayer where a "qualified" man is present, she is required to wear a head covering to show her submission.

Stupid me—I had been taught to respect the elders—I gave honest answers. After no doubt getting off on the salacious details, the committee judged that I was not repentant, a condition of forgiveness and reinstatement. Appealing their decision and pleading my case to the governing body in New York was a no-go.

Things got worse when the congregation split between supporters of Ken, and supporters of me. Because I was the one who left home, the elders accused me of creating a division—another major No-No.

I was not present when the dreaded Letter of Disfellowshipping was read from the podium: "This person has engaged in behavior not befitting a Christian and is to be shunned." And, quoting from the Bible, "...do not receive this person into your house nor greet them; for he who greets such a one shares his evil deeds."

As devout as my mother was, she took the shunning very seriously and all-but stopped having anything to do with me.

Luckily, disfellowshipping did not affect our move to Rick's place. He was already disfellowshipped—for the second time—and had no interest in being reinstated. I, on the other hand, did everything that was required of me, which meant attending all the public meetings for a year, sitting in the back row at the Kingdom Hall, not speaking or being spoken to.

For me, that year meant being cut off from the only support system I knew (inadequate though it had proven to be), while facing a divorce with virtually no money and three young kids, one of them a behavioral nightmare, and no home of our own.

Ken's attorney offered me child support of $75/month per child and $75/month alimony, which even in 1981was laughable. However, as I was ignorant of the fact that I could have gotten my own lawyer and negotiated a more reasonable divorce settlement, I accepted it.

At this point, I understood why my mother had been tempted to jump in front of that train when my dad dumped us. I spent a significant amount of time wishing myself dead and thinking about how best to do it. But as someone who actually attempted suicide pointed out to me, we find so many reasons not to die. My reason was that nobody would take care of my kids and I wasn't about to leave them alone and defenseless.

I considered checking into a mental health facility, but for the same reason, I didn't. As hard as it was, looking back, I'm glad. Being compelled to deal with it all made me stronger. Please be sure I am not suggesting that everyone in that position should feel they have to make the same choice, but for me, it was the right one. And I would not want to have to make it again.

Those elders had taken everything from me, I thought one morning as I was tidying the kids' room. That thought was followed by an *aha!* moment: There was still something they could never access. My private thoughts would always be mine and mine alone.

An old Louis Armstrong song became my mantra.

> *The way you wear your hat*
> *The way you sip your tea*
> *The memory of all that*
> *No no they can't take that away from me.*

Chapter 44

A turning point

My first experience with therapy came when I was thirty-one. A friend persuaded me to make an appointment with the therapist who had helped him through some serious personal trauma. Telling my friend that the 100-mile round trip had better be worth it, I went to Roland Sparks' office in Laguna Beach.

Greeting me warmly at the door with the twinkly eyes of a middle-aged elf, Roland showed me to the sofa. Fidgeting with my hands, not at all sure what to expect, I sat silent, wondering how to begin.

"How can I help you, my dear?" asked the therapist.

Wasn't he *supposed to tell* me *that?*

I shrugged helplessly. "I don't know. I'm just an ordinary housewife. I don't even know why I'm here. I don't drink, don't smoke or do drugs; I don't sleep around."

Roland chuckled. "Would you like me to bring in someone to beat you up?"

What did he just say?

"Of course not," I sputtered. "Why would you say that?"

"Why do you want to be abused?" he asked.

Was he crazy?

"I don't want to be abused!"

Then he asked the question that led to me changing my life: "Why do you keep putting yourself in situations where you are abused?"

At first I didn't get it. But in that fifty-minute session I came to recognize that he was absolutely right—I *had* put myself into the abusive situation I had just left, after staying in for too many years.

Just as importantly, I learned that I had been depressed since I was ten. Oh. That was when we first left England. Go figure. But wait—isn't depression a temporary state caused by a specific situation? Surprise! It turned out that someone can have underlying depression all the time. For *years*. And that someone was me. Low-level depressed for twenty-one years...

Leaving Roland's office that day, for the first time in—maybe ever—I got my first taste of hope—a sense that I was on the road to something better—way, way better. It wasn't going to come easy, but it was going to come.

The hundred-mile weekly round trip was oh-so worth it. Thank you, George, for pushing me into it.

Chapter 45

I can make something happen

At the end of my year of being disfellowshipped I applied and was approved for reinstatement. To be reinstated meant that at the end of the year, the committee judged the sinner—me—for a second time and they believed in my sincere repentance for my evil deeds; that I had turned around, and was no longer sinning.

There's nothing the JW brothers and sisters like better than a reinstatement. The congregation welcomed me back into the flock with arms open wide. Honestly, it felt good to be back in the fold. For a while, anyway.

Then, four years later, it happened all over again.

After moving in with Rick and Sandy, I worked part-time as office manager at a small restaurant manufacturing shop. I was the only female keeping an eye on a rowdy bunch of carpenters constructing tables and booths. My favorites were the do-rag wearing bikers. They were the nicest guys and showed me respect, even when they were goofing off. Tim, the toughest of them all, made a wooden sign for the restroom I exclusively used. It read "WOMAN."

As any single parent knows, especially with multiple kids, keeping everything going takes a lot out of a person. For someone whose own parents were a little short in the discipline department, even more so. I was just winging it.

One Friday, I left them all in the station wagon and went into the shop to pick up my check. Not five minutes later, Bonnie came running in to report that Erik had found a flare in the emergency kit and lit it in the car! Once again, Rick to the rescue! Luckily, my brother was also working at the shop that day, and prevented the potential conflagration.

Erik was the middle kid who tried to convince me he was Spiderman by constantly wearing the costume and literally climbing the walls. When he was three, he jumped off the top of the fridge and broke his front teeth. The second time, he was ten, riding the handlebars of a friend's bike.

That Saturday evening, I had the dubious honor of assisting the dentist as he reimplanted Erik's tooth. That kid was always up to something. These days, he rides motorcycles and drives a fast Mustang. As a child, he released his frustrations by drawing some pretty scary scenes. As a teen, after he cobbled together a tattoo machine and put his first skin art on his little brother, I bought him some real equipment. He developed his skills and grew into a talented tattoo artist.

Ben, the youngest, was quiet and shy—the good child. He wrote poetry and songs, and with his friend, Henry, got into music. First, they called themselves +NRG. Henry was Henna-C and Ben was, and still is, known as Stoli Michaels. He did some modeling and some dancing.

From an introverted little guy, my baby grew up to be a rock star in Europe, performing as part of *Snap!* For many years, he's been the rapper for singer, Penny Ford. If you know the song, *"I've Got the Power,"* it may be Ben you are hearing. Oh, and he's the father of my only grandchild, the amazing and impressive Cleo.

As for Bonnie/Jennifer, if ever there was a troubled soul it was my daughter. Being the eldest, she bore the brunt of the chaotic household she was born into. She was smart, though, and learned to read fifty words before she turned two. I've detailed in another chapter the difficulties I had with her early on, and they didn't improve after she returned from the group home in Utah.

Getting her to school was a nightmare. Even when she showed up, she often walked out of class and went, well, wherever she wanted to. One morning she was lying in bed watching TV, refusing to get dressed. I followed through on my threat to remove the TV—a bulky CRT monster. As I was carrying it out of her room, Bonnie jumped on my back, arms around my neck. She was fourteen and nearly as big as me.

When I told Roland about it in my next therapy session he made a remark that stuck with me. "If she doesn't get hold of herself, one of these days, someone is going to rise up and smack her in the chops."

Most of the time, I felt like a little boat with no oars, being tossed about on the ocean waves in a storm. I was driving home from work one day, depressed and struggling with the *crisis du jour*. I sighed loudly and said, "Oh well, I guess I'll see what happens next."

Suddenly, as if a lightning bolt hit me (sorry about the cliché), I had an epiphany. A voice in my head said, "You don't have to wait for something to happen. You can *make* something happen."

It may sound ludicrous, but for me, that realization was an important turning point on my path to independence. Akin to recognizing my saturation point with Ken, it was a major step along the road.

I applied for Section 8 Housing, a program where the government contributed part of the rent for people who qualify. With my small part-time income and three children, I definitely qualified. There was, discouragingly, a year-long waiting, but my dad advised me to sign up because, as he said, "The time is going to pass anyway."

Happily, I took his advice, and months sooner than expected, got approved for a small three-bedroom house in La Puente. Not the best neighborhood, but not the worst, either. More than a year after Rick took us in, the kids and I moved to Gemini Street.

Dad was working at JC Penney, winning prizes in furniture sales. He sneaked a couple of items over to my new home—a brass lamp with a slight dent, a rug. It wasn't that he was sneaking them from Penney's; he bought them. The sneaking was so Roslyn wouldn't know. She and Dad came to dinner one evening and she took me aside.

"I just want you to know," said my stepmother, "Your father and I are not going to help you in any way."

I stared at her for a long moment, unsure if I had heard correctly. If I'd been British enough, I would have said something like, "Piss off, you mad cow." But by then, I knew her well enough that it was not a big surprise that she would say such a rotten thing. Knowing it hurt me when she referred to me as 'the bad news bear,' she did it frequently. I admit there was a lot of bad news in my life those days.

Chapter 46
Oops, it happened again

I met a man through my job. He was an architect whose wife had moved out one day, leaving him with their three kids—they were the same ages as mine. It was never quite a relationship, but whatever you called it, it was a diversion from the daily grind, and provided some excitement for a frazzled 34-year-old single mom.

From time to time, my boss used to send me in his little truck to deliver materials to our guys working on a remodeling project at the Mondrian Hotel in West Hollywood. Once or twice, the architect met me there. We'd get into the elevator and between floors he would press the STOP button for a few romantic moments. He knew which suites were unoccupied, and knowing we could have been caught *in flagrante delicto* added an piquant element of adventure.

The affair lasted a short few months before guilt overcame both of us. He was a Mormon high priest and I was still trying to be a JW. For both of us, that meant sex outside of marriage was *verboten*, even when it was very, very good. Maybe especially then…

We broke it off, but because it's no good trying to be a half-JW, I went and confessed to the elders that I'd been in a 'dating' relationship. This was a different congregation from last time, but my records had followed me and the elders were aware of my murky past. The committee met and decided that I was 'clearly a danger to the congregation.' I needed to be cut out like a malignant tumor.

So, on my thirty-fifth birthday, I was disfellowshipped for the second time.

My spirit guides had finally hit me over the head hard enough with a two-by-four that I finally saw the light and never went back.

I can say in all honesty and with great enthusiasm that being ignominiously booted from the JW cult is one of the very best things that has ever happened to me. That notwithstanding, as I had spent twenty-seven years being brainwashed that Jehovah's Witnesses had 'the truth,' it took no less than *fifteen years* to wipe my psyche completely clean of them.

Twenty-five years later I published *Last Writes*, the fourth title in my "Forensic Handwriting" mystery/suspense series. I think of it as my 're-venge' book. I created a religious cult and called it the *Temple of Brighter Light.* Here's why: Whenever the JW governing body makes a prediction that doesn't come true, they excuse their error by saying, "the light is always getting brighter." In other words, "we weren't yet seeing the full picture." Not "we screwed up."

A good example is found in the years leading up to 1975. We JWs were told in no uncertain terms and many times over that this was going to be the year we would see an end to "this system of things" (i.e., the world as we know it). It was strongly implied that Armageddon—God's war between good and evil—would arrive and only JWs would be saved from the worldwide destruction that was about to take place.

Based on an obscure mathematical formula devised to come up with this date, the Witnesses were instructed to put their lives on hold—don't buy homes or get an education, or start a family. This messed up a lot of people, attested to by similar stories posted by thousands of members of various XJW (ex-Jehovah's Witness) Facebook pages.

As we all know, 1975 came and went, and no Armageddon. As was typical, the Borg, as we apostates like to call the organization—If you're a Trekkie, you'll get the reference—blamed the obedient members, claiming they had misinterpreted what had been said.

Unquestioning loyalty is built into JW DNA, so the poor, blind sheeple were willing to accept the blame without question, Ken and me among them. Even in a state of dementia, my 94-year-old mother continues to accept, unconditionally, anything they tell her.

When I wrote *Last Writes,* I swiped a direct quote from a JW publication that says everything you need to know about their philosophy:

> *"Brothers, we would not want to engage in*
> *independent thinking."*

Thank God that those weekly therapy sessions with Roland Sparks were teaching me independent thinking.

Chapter 47

Exit points

Around eleven o'clock one night my stepmother called, hysterical.

"There's been a terrible accident," Roslyn's words were running together. I had to strain to understand what she was saying. "Your father's trapped in the bathroom and we don't know whether he's dead or alive."

If you don't think those words can chill the blood in your veins, you're lucky not to have had such an experience.

My mother lived close enough to come and stay with the kids. Putting the pedal to the metal, I tore up the fifteen miles to San Dimas in a cold sweat, not knowing what I was going to find.

As I came down Lone Hill Avenue I saw people standing out in the street, and a fire truck. I scanned the crowd around where the stucco wall was supposed to be that normally surrounded the back part of the house, and broke down in tears. There was my dad in a big black parka with fur trim around the hood. I was so grateful to be able to give him a hug.

A drunk teenage girl in her boyfriend's two-week-old Camaro had barreled down Lone Hill at speed. The house was at the end of a Tee, where you had to make a left or right turn at Cypress. Failing to notice the Stop sign, the girl had plowed across the road and straight through the wall. The vehicle slewed to the right and exploded through the sliding glass door that led into the master bedroom, ending up on the king-sized bed.

The back half of the house looked like a bomb had hit it. Roslyn had been in the kitchen. Dad had just stepped into the bathroom, which was where he was trapped. The fire department had to unblock the door to get him out.

It was a Saturday night and my little sister was out partying. That was long before cell phones; there was no way to call and alert her. When things had calmed down and the neighbors were back in their homes, Dad and Roslyn retired to the guestroom, while I sat up all night in the front room, waiting for Sara to walk through the door. It was nearly six a.m. when she finally came in, stunned by the sight that met her.

In my afterlife studies since my daughter's murder, I've learned that before we come to the earth we have the opportunity to set up several potential exit points. I would not be surprised if this event was one of my dad's, and at the last minute he opted out.

Another possible example is my ex-brother-in-law and close friend, Doug. He was hospitalized with acute appendicitis and nearly died. But he recovered. About two years later, four years after Jen's murder, he was riding his bicycle one morning. A woman parked on the street opened her car door without looking and knocked Doug off his bike. He hit his head and it could have been serious, but that day, he was okay.

Doug owned a Harley motorcycle and a Mustang (yes, we were a Mustang family) that he liked to drive fast. Yet, a week after being knocked off his bicycle, he was once again out riding it when he was hit by a car and killed. Were those earlier events exit points that Doug ignored? I can only conjecture.

As a left-brained logical engineer who worked on the Space Shuttle, he had a hard time accepting anything without tangible proof. After we lost Jen—Doug and she were very close—he *wanted* to believe in the Afterlife, but he was never quite sure.

I gave him a very left-brained book by Dr. Gary Schwartz—*The Afterlife Experiments: Breakthrough Scientific Evidence of Life After Death*. Doug ate it up, but he stopped short of being able to say that he believed in the Afterlife.

He was a tall man and broad, with the biggest laugh you ever heard. Coming from a repressive household, he had difficulty verbalizing his deeper emotions, and they came out in this huge, uncontrollable laugh—it made you want to laugh with him.

After Doug was killed I attended a group session at the medium Brian Hurst's home. During the session, Brian brought through someone who'd had a strong impact to the head—a man who had been hit while riding a bicycle. Then he actually said the name Doug and mentioned a very hearty laugh. He told Brian that he wanted me to know he had changed his tune about the Afterlife.

The exit point my dad eventually chose came a year and a half after the incident with the girl who drove into his house.

I was temping at a Bank of America office. My supervisor came to let me know I had a personal phone call. Who on earth knew where to find me? Mystified, I picked up the phone. Sara was on the line, crying. "We lost daddy in the night and we don't know what to do."

Ten minutes later, sitting alone in my old Datsun B210 in the parking garage, I screamed and screamed, a primal release of years of accumulated anger and frustration and grief.

My dad was sixty-three and obese, with all the health problems that come with being overweight—diabetes, high blood pressure, gout, etc. For all his yelling, he was basically a peacemaker who tried unsuccessfully to moderate between Roslyn and Sara, Roslyn and Rick, Roslyn and me. Bottom line, his wife was a troublemaker who was not happy unless she was stirring things up.

A week before he went to sleep and never woke up, my father called and asked me to talk to her. As was frequently the case, she had been her usual horrible self to me and we were not on speaking terms.

"Just one more time," Dad pleaded. "For my sake."

More than once he had called on me for help when Sara and her mother were about to come to blows in a serious way. I had done my best to calm things down each of those times. This time, Roslyn had hit the limits of my patience. I was done. I turned down my dad's request and refused to speak with her, even for his sake.

And now there would be no more chances.

The last time I saw him alive, six weeks earlier, he had met me for lunch.

He was on sick leave, recovering from a stroke. His first stroke had hit around fifteen years earlier in his late forties. Although he was not physically affected in the long term, each attack on his body changed his personality a little more, draining the essence of who he had been. He was no longer the jokester I had known all my life.

When he'd turned sixty I asked him to write a handwriting sample for me. What he chose to write is, in my mind, an apology of sorts for leaving us, his first family:

> "I wonder why life is so complicated. In the face of it, it seems simple, but one must consider that different lives are interwoven and therefore what one does affects people. So one should consider one's action before one acts.

I wish I would have been around to see my daughter and son Richard grow up, but it's a joy to have them around now."

His remorse extended to my mother. During his hospitalization he had asked to see her, perhaps to make amends. Rick and I snuck her in for a visit when Roslyn wasn't there.

Over lunch he talked about his desire to return home to England and be with his three sisters. He had always been independent, but while he was ailing, Roslyn had taken control of the purse strings and was keeping them shut tight. What she didn't know was, Dad's family across the pond were secretly plotting a reverse kidnapping. They were devising a way to bring him home and keep him there.

"What are you going to do now?" I asked, watching him across the table; he seemed so sad and lost. "Do you have some goals?"

He slowly shook his head. "Not really."

"You have to have goals," I said naively. "Life isn't worth living without them."

"You're right," said my dad. When we parted in the parking lot he hugged me as if he knew he would never see me again.

He arrived home to the heartbreaking news from England that his closest sister, my Auntie Rosie, had died suddenly. Six weeks later, he followed her.

That was long before I learned about exit points.

Chapter 48

Worth more than $8/hour

I t never occurred to me that my skills were worth more than the $8/hour I was making as a temp secretary and word processor.

I learned it from man named Simon Cohen, a private graphology student who had been introduced to me by another student. Si was an entrepreneur who had been a designer of women's shoes and owned a shoe factory in Italy. Now, he was a real estate broker with an office in West L.A and was fascinated by handwriting analysis.

As he got into his studies and we got better acquainted, Si saw something in me that he wanted to exploit. His vision was to mold me and to make me grow and flourish in the field. You might say, he fancied himself as Henry Higgins to my Eliza Doolittle.

He took me to a Beverly Hills hairstylist who styled and colored my hair. When the stylist turned the chair around and I looked in the mirror I felt like a movie star. New clothes, instructions on how to sell myself as a handwriting analyst. It was all pretty heady. For about five minutes, anyway. In his way, Si was as much of an abuser as my husband had been. He became a difficult but important force along my spiritual path.

Before long, Si was pressing for more than a student/teacher relationship. I was ambivalent about getting involved—the JW hooks were still strong in me—but I went out to dinner with him, and that was the start of a three-year partnership.

Shortly before that first date, I was complaining about a much older man who was coming on to me.

"How old do you think I am?" Si asked, amused.

"Forty-five?" I guessed, hoping I wasn't insulting him. It was a shock to learn that he was a year younger than my father—61. I was in my mid-thirties.

He looked a bit like Frank Sinatra and had an ageless kind of crackling energy. He was as charming as he was profoundly angry.

Sometime he was just plain mean; it seemed to come naturally. "You're the biggest disappointment in my life," he once told me when I wasn't as compliant as he would have liked.

He told me about being a nineteen-year-old Air Force navigator in WWII.

"I was shot down twice over France," Si said.

I can be a good listener and he was a good storyteller. He told me about the farmer and his family who took him in after he was shot down, and how they nursed him for weeks, treating his shrapnel-peppered legs. As soon as he was able, Si left the farm and started a trek across the Pyrenees, avoiding Franco's men as best he could. He blamed the terrible things he witnessed— like Nazis soldiers savagely blinding a Jewish doctor—for his extreme irritability and impatience. "I have no tolerance for bullshit," he was fond of saying.

The realtors who came to work in the office admired him, some loved him, and most quickly left. Nobody wanted to work under his negativity for long.

When we became partners we set up *The Graphology Center*—a big name for a little business. The back room of Si's real estate offices became a classroom where I taught the basics of handwriting analysis. Several of those students became good friends.

When I wasn't teaching or lecturing, I was writing technical papers about handwriting and looking for ways to market my services. Without the Internet, that was much harder than it is today.

One year, Si and I co-hosted a conference cruise and took seventy-seven handwriting analysts to Mexico. The travel agent, who had promised to be with us all the way and handle any problems, met us at the ship and said, 'I'm not going with you after all—seeya.' And then we met the woman who was going to be the bookseller for the event. She was so obnoxious that by the end of the first day, Si had to be restrained from tossing her overboard. And then we sat down to dinner and I got seasick. Somehow, though, everyone managed to have a good time.

The captain, Demitrius Mylonas, invited us to sit at his table for the gala banquet. Before knowing Si, I would never have dreamed of spending $300 on a dress. Wearing a sequined black gown, I felt confident enough to ask Captain Mylonas for his handwriting. The signature he gave me is one I still use in my lectures—you can read his name, but it looks just like a ship sailing on the ocean.

Si took me for my very first psychic reading to a woman named Sandra. It was exciting and scary for me, defying what I had been taught for so many years—that psychic phenomena was demonic. I'm happy to report that no demons came home with me after that visit. Or any other.

The one thing that stuck with me from that reading is what Sandra said about my daughter: "She's like a wounded deer in the forest. Somebody has to rescue her or shoot her." I know she was speaking metaphorically, but fifteen years later, Jennifer was shot to death.

Chapter 49

Going to court

I was in the Graphology Center office when a call came from an attorney who was suing his son-in-law. He claimed the guy had forged a signature on an agreement.

"I don't do that kind of work," I told him. "I do personality assessment."

"Do you know handwriting?" he asked.

"Yes," I said. "I've been in practice for nearly twenty years."

And then came yet another of those turning points that changed the trajectory of my life.

"I'll get you qualified," said the attorney. "We're going to court tomorrow."

$\int$

I wore a tweed jacket that Si had persuaded me to buy at a high-end second-hand store—he had impeccable and expensive taste, but he knew how to find a bargain. For the first time ever, I found myself perched on the edge of a chair on the witness stand.

I probably should have been more stressed, but I didn't know enough to be. Staying up late into the night, I had studied the documents the attorney had hand-delivered for me to examine. I'd consulted with a colleague who had some experience in handwriting authentication, and she told me what to do. I was as ready as I could be.

When an expert witness takes the stand, the first thing that happens is *voir dire.* This is a preliminary examination of a witness to determine whether or not they are qualified to testify. After listening to the questions and answers, the judge gets to decide.

My attorney-client asked a bunch of questions about my education and experience. That was easy enough, and I was sailing along, feeling good. Then things came to a screeching halt, when he asked, "Ms. Lowe, is there a hierarchy of opinions in document examination?"

This was something I had read about the night before in my prep. "Yes," I answered confidently.

"Would you please tell us what those opinion levels are and explain them."

That's when I froze. Breaking protocol and not knowing I was, I turned to the judge. "I'm so sorry your honor, but my mind has gone blank."

Knowing this was my first time to testify, the judge smiled. "Don't worry," he said. "It happens to all of us." Then he nodded at the attorneys. "She's qualified."

In case you are curious, the hierarchy of opinions that I currently use is a seven-level scale published by the Scientific Association of Forensic Examiners (pssst—I am one of its authors). It goes like this, from left to right:

Elimination: the person can be eliminated as the author of the signature or other writing)
Strong **probability:** the writing is not genuine
Probably not genuine
Inconclusive: not enough evidence to decide either way
Probably genuine
Strong **probability** the writing is genuine
Identification: the person can be identified as the author

The attorney won his case. I think I charged him $25. Today, a court appearance would cost him closer to $2000.

Following that experience I took several courses in document examination and learned from some of the best in the field. This aspect of handwriting analysis has become my main area of work. No matter how many times I've testified (more than 70), getting on the witness stand continues to be the most stressful part of my practice. As a colleague once said, it's the opposing attorney's job to make the expert look stupid. It's the expert's job not to help.

I've learned that's not always easy to do.

In several cases when I was testifying for the defense in criminal trials, especially female prosecutors were pretty tricky. Maybe it's because they feel they need to be more assertive than their male counterparts. I don't believe that's a good excuse to try and put one over on the jury.

In one case, the ADA (assistant district attorney) purported to be quoting from my website, and what she said seemed to contradict my testimony. The smart thing would have been for me to ask her to let me see the piece of paper she was reading from. But I was so taken aback that I just replied that if what she had said was on my website it would need to be changed. Later, I discovered that what she had read was not from my site at all. Luckily, the jury saw through her obfuscation.

What I learned from that experience stood me in good stead in another case.

The defense attorney I was working for introduced me to the prosecutor during the lunch break, after which I was to be called to the stand. I had printed a color copy of my demonstrative exhibits with parts of the illustrations in red so they would stand out. The ADA asked me to let her copy the exhibit and she would return it after lunch. I didn't trust her, but at the direction of the attorney I was working for, I reluctantly complied.

After lunch, as I was walking to the witness stand, the ADA shoved some papers at me. When I started to refer to them, I found that she had returned, not my copies, but a black and white set, which didn't have the effect they needed to. On the stand, I pointed out that she had given me the wrong copies. From her seat at the counsel table the prosecutor gave a knowing smile and shrugged.

Explaining to the judge that it was important for the jury to see the color illustrations, I requested to show them my laptop (the courtroom equipment I would normally use wasn't available). Lucky for me I had brought the laptop, which I usually don't do. And lucky for me, the judge said yes.

I booted up and launched PowerPoint. After asking for permission to step down from the witness stand, I walked up and down in front of the jury box, showing them on the screen what they needed to see and explaining why the ADA was wrong.

The young woman defendant who was being falsely accused of a crime was acquitted, and I felt pretty damn self-satisfied.

Chapter 50

Oprah takes on Bonnie

The kids went to live in Utah with their father for a while—a tremendous wrench for all of us. Bonnie's rebellious, impossible behavior had become more than I could manage, and the family therapist we were seeing suggested it was time for Ken to step up. I followed what turned out to be terrible advice, and paid the price.

I was in the Graphology Center office one afternoon when I got a phone call from my ten-year-old son, Erik. "Daddy's in jail and Bonnie's in the hospital and Ben and me are home alone and we don't know what to do."

Typing those words brings back the sickening helpless fear of being seven-hundred miles away from my kids when they needed me. My vision went blurry and my heart was racing. *What the hell had happened?*

Nobody had told me Bonnie had run away from home a week or so earlier. The day Erik phoned, she had showed up at school and the school officials called her father. The police report (let it be said that Ken denies this) indicates that he entered the room where they were holding her and locked the door behind him. Watching through the window while someone was frantically searching for a key, they say they saw him push her to the floor and start hitting her. When they got the door opened, he is said to have turned and said, "Did you see what she did to me?" Which reminded me of the times in the past when he denied the threats he had made.

He was released from police custody and Bonnie was placed in a group home, where she stayed for the next year, while I did everything I could to get her released and bring her back home. At that group home, she was introduced to pot and other drugs.

This was a period so painful and difficult that I resist thinking about it in any detail.

She was thirteen when she came home, and was positive she would not live to see her eighteenth birthday. If my daughter's behavior was unruly and difficult before she went to Utah, now it was completely out of control. She started climbing out of the window at night to meet her friends and go to the graveyard—for what, I can only conjecture, and I don't want to.

The Ouija board became a bone of contention. I was still under the influence of my JW upbringing, and when I found a note that she told me had been written by a spirit named Zulp, I was convinced that the demons were active in our house (shades of my mother).

Meanwhile, Ben and Erik, still in Utah, were miserable. Erik wrote me a letter telling me that Ben, who was only seven, was crying in his sleep. I kept it, but I cannot bring myself to read it. When they came to visit for the summer their suitcases were packed with every item of clothing they owned, hoping to move back home.

There was so much wrong with their living arrangement that finally, as difficult as it was to be a single mom without a decent income, I brought them home to stay.

Then Bonnie went on the Oprah show.

An old friend and colleague, Jeanette Farmer, was acquainted with Dr. Ken Magid, who had written a well-regarded book, *High Risk: Children Without a Conscience*. Jeanette had done some handwriting analysis work for him, and when he was invited to appear on Oprah, it was suggested that a 'difficult'

child should appear with him. Knowing the problems I had with Bonnie, Jeanette suggested her.

I asked her if she wanted to go, and she decided that she did. For a fourteen-year-old, I suppose the idea of flying to Chicago to be on a famous TV show held a certain appeal. As averse as I am to air travel, Rick offered to chaperone her, which basically meant stopping her from getting into the mini bottles of booze in the hotel room fridge.

When I dropped them at LAX, Bonnie yelled at me in her usual rude fashion. Her default was, "I hate you, you f***ing bitch," and it somehow got reported to the show. Oprah asked her on-air why she did that. She shrugged and said nothing. I'm not sure she opened her mouth during the entire segment. They had me on the phone to the studio, but I have zero recollection of what I was asked or answered.

It was a mistake to send her; I saw that afterwards. One of the many I made.

After Oprah, Ken's parents wouldn't let the kids in their house. Her appearance alone was enough to embarrass this intensely private family. Mind you, Bonnie didn't say *anything* about their family, negative or otherwise, nor about anything else. She just sat on the stage, glowering.

Chapter 51

Oh, those cards

I met Bob Joseph while on my way to a board meeting in northern California. I'd stopped off in Ojai, a charming spiritual and artistic village. Bob was doing psychic tarot card readings at the Heart of Light bookstore, and I booked a session.

This was only my second reading. I was still in the process of shedding my old JW skin. When Bob told me that a man with an "R" name was coming from the east coast to visit me I nearly fell off my chair. Roger Rubin, mentor and friend, was soon to arrive from New York.

After that, I pestered Bob on an almost-daily basis. I don't know how he stood it, but he never complained about my myriad calls as I whined about my many problems with the kids and, shortly after, with Bill. He eventually taught me how to read tarot for myself, which didn't stop me from constantly calling to ask whether I'd got it right.

I had always wanted to write a mystery—my choice of reading genre. Eight years after I met Bob I started writing *Poison Pen*. There is a saying, "Write what you know." So, I created a character who did the same kind of work as me, and named her Claudia Rose. A woman I knew who had recently died under mysterious circumstances was known to have had some 'interesting' sexual proclivities. I used them to develop the plot. My first book, *The Complete Idiot's Guide to Handwriting Analysis* was published and doing well, but there is a huge difference between writing nonfiction and fiction. I didn't know what I was doing.

Until he started giving me writing advice, I had no idea that Robert Joseph was the author of eleven novels by Random House, some published under a pseudonym, and a cookbook. One of his books reportedly sold a half-million copies!

I was happy to drive every week or so from L.A. to Bob's house in Ventura to read twenty pages of my story aloud for him to critique. He had loads of good ideas for me to incorporate, and he wasn't shy about telling me when something was crap. He has been my first listener for every one of my books since. In my book (literally), this man should be nominated for sainthood.

For more than thirty years, Bob has continued to be a good and dear friend, sticking with me throughout my two marriages and two divorces from Bill, and everything else. He was also a friend to Jennifer, and was at her funeral, holding me up.

As a psychic, his insight and experience has proven invaluable. Even after moving out of state, he continues to listen to me, helping me along my spiritual path with patience and compassion.

Chapter 52

The Boz

Kids are expensive to raise. When temp work wasn't cutting it, I took a full-time job at Western Federal Savings as executive assistant to the manager of the warehouse where all the branches stored extra equipment and furniture. The company's properties were managed from our office, and supplies ordered.

In the eighteen months I was employed there I felt part of a close-knit family. I loved that job and the people I worked with. And then our wonderful boss got pushed out and a manipulative schemer took his place. The new guy offered to keep me on at the same salary but with a reduced title of Senior Secretary. He was clearly surprised when I said, "No thanks. I quit."

I found another "assistant to the administrator" position at Bosley Medical Group, a Beverly Hills hair transplant clinic. That's where I spent another eighteen months of my life; another place where I made some long-term friends. But working for Dr. Bosley was not good for one's mental health. Look up "super-controlling angry man" in the dictionary and you will find his picture right next to Simon Cohen's. How did I keep finding these men?!

During the time I worked at BMG, 'the Boz,' as we called him, went through no less than *nine* very well-paid executive secretaries. The quickest one left after a mere two hours after learning that part of the job description was for her to meet the Boz in the parking garage and carry his dry cleaning up to the fifth floor penthouse. Oh, and that she would have to make his lunch. That was where she drew the line.

Dr. Bosley had a thing about names. When I came on board, his assistant's name had been Michaela.

"Oh, no," he declared. "That's too strange; I can't remember that. From now on, her name is Kelly." Then, Kelly Van Ness was hired to work on the fourth floor at the front desk. "Oh, no," he said. "We can't have two Kellys, that's too confusing. Her name is now Vanessa." And then four Kathys were hired. You can probably guess what happened next. Almost nobody in the front office got to keep their own name. I like to think that I would have refused to give up mine.

Every time one of Dr. Bosley's assistants quit, I was sent to the penthouse to substitute until he hired his next victim, er, assistant. On those days, I was taking Xanax by nine a.m. in order to make it through. Thankfully, he often took time off to go skiing in Vale, or fly his Cessna to Colorado and I could relax.

One morning he told me he needed a ride to pick up his Bentley (whose license plate read "Ruffnit") at the repair shop. The thought of him shoe-horning his six-foot frame into my beat-up old Datsun was mortifying. But to his credit, the Boz didn't complain. He did say I was an aggressive driver, which, from him, was a high compliment.

We finally found him the perfect secretary through handwriting analysis. After narrowing down the four hundred applications (yes, I'm serious), there were two excellent candidates.

It goes without saying that Dr. Bosley ignored my advice on which one to pick—Maria, the one who was not going to put up with his shenanigans. Instead, he hired Eileen, who had excellent skills, but didn't have Maria's backbone.

Eileen started work and the Boz liked her as much as he could like anyone. And then, six months later, she couldn't stomach him anymore and one day while he was out of town, quit without notice.

As usual, I was sent to Eileen's office in the penthouse. When the Boz arrived and heard that she had quit, he was furious. "Why would she do that?" he demanded in high dudgeon. "Why would she leave me without giving notice?"

I pointed out that all staff members had recently been coerced into signing an Employment at Will form. We could now be terminated without notice and without cause, and, likewise, we had the right to quit without notice.

That wasn't good enough for Dr. Bosley. Several times that morning he returned to my desk looking puzzled, asking me the same question: Why?

In the end, I wearied of it and told him the truth as Eileen had related it to me. "Eileen was raped in her apartment by a stranger. She said that coming here to work for you every day gave her the same feeling."

The Boz listened, and when I was done, he said, "Huh," and walked away. A few minutes later he returned, shaking his head.

"I don't get it," he said. "Men go off to war and see their buddies killed; they get over it. A woman has sex maybe 10,000 times in her life. Can't she forget just one time?"

And that, I decided, was the reason he couldn't keep an assistant.

I suggested we contact Maria, who I had lobbied for all those months ago, to see if she might still be interested in the job. She was, he hired her, and all was well in the penthouse. As well as it could be.

When something annoyed the Boz he would red-faced yell about it, sometimes yelling about a patient while standing right outside that person's examining room. Once, he yelled at me. I turned on him with my sternest Mom glare, and in my coldest tone, said, "Don't you *ever* talk to me like that again."

He never did. But maybe that little display of defiance contributed to my being fired not too long afterward. The day after I lost my job, that poor old blue Datsun died a death from which there could be no resurrection.

My kids were 12, 14, and 17, and I had rent and credit card debt to pay. What better time to go into business for myself?

The only way I can explain why I decided to do just that is that my spirit guides (who I hadn't yet met) were whispering in my ear.

Chapter 53

The Write Choice!

With no wheels and no income, I walked down to the local Hyundai dealer—they had the cheapest cars around and I was desperate. Before there was time for them to find out that I was no longer gainfully employed, I agreed to a deal at a usury interest rate. The interest over the five-year loan cost more than the damn car. And within six weeks that piece of crap needed new struts and the battery blew up.

So, now I had a new car and excellent administrative skills and experience in the corporate world. I re-signed with a temp agency so I could pay the bills while building up my handwriting analysis practice. Having been my avocation and side gig for two decades, how hard could it be to go full time?

I haunted the local print shop, ordering business cards and brochures, and creating marketing collateral for my new entity: Sheila Lowe & Associates, *the Write Choice!* I sent letters to companies, selling the benefits of handwriting analysis and asking for a meeting.

Regretfully, it was not the walk in the park I had envisioned. Most of the business owners I approached didn't see why they needed my services. Once in a while, I would get an appointment with someone who was willing to listen.

Marketing to temp agencies was my best bet. They employed a sales force, and handwriting analysis could help them hire people who were most likely to succeed. Plus, having worked for several agencies, I spoke their lingo. My pitch was: it's not a lack of skills that cause most people to fail in a position, it's personality traits, which can be identified in handwriting.

Kathryn Shepherd owned a temp agency, and she gave this nervous handwriting analyst her first real break. She not only hired me to analyze handwritings for her own prospective employees, she invited me to speak at a conference of the California Association of Personnel Consultants, where I acquired additional clients.

It was slow going, but I was on my way, and there were always the helpers, like Kath, and one of her referrals, Carl Miller. I realize that's not quite the context Mr. Rogers meant when he told children to "look for the helpers," but for me, that's what these people were.

δ

Si Cohen moved away and we closed the Graphology Center. I began teaching handwriting analysis classes in my apartment and gave lectures at practically every Lions Club and Rotary club that existed in the greater Los Angeles area. Libraries, too, and just about any other venue seeking a speaker. Everyone was interested in learning about their handwriting.

Another strong client came through Mary Ruiz. Along with Karen Amend, Mary had co-authored *Handwriting Analysis, The Complete Basic Book*, a favorite of mine when I was learning my craft. She was also a member of the Los Angeles Chapter of the American Handwriting Analysis Foundation, which I had founded.

When Mary was diagnosed with cancer, she asked me to take on a client of hers who owned a busy dude ranch. Tragically, she died within a year of her diagnosis. I remain eternally grateful for the steady work that came through that contact.

Even with these new clients my practice was not progressing at the pace I thought it should. I turned, as I so often did, to Bob Joseph for a psychic reading. He laid out a card spread and talked about what he saw. He said something that shocked me.

"Are you sure you want to do this? You're not really committed to it."

It was like a replay of that moment when Roland Sparks asked, "Why do you put yourself in a position to be abused?" Total bewilderment that led to one of those critical turning points.

"What do you mean?" I sputtered, just as I had to Roland. "All these months I've been working my butt off, giving lectures and teaching and meeting with potential clients. How can I be more committed than that?"

But as we talked further, I realized Bob was right. I was going through all the right motions, but in my heart, I never expected to succeed.

Not long after that conversation, a friend suggested I read a small book published in 1925 called *The Game of Life and How to Play* it by Florence Scovel Shinn. It's about the Law of Attraction—how to use our thoughts to bring positive results into our lives. Today, the principles it outlines are known as '*The Secret.*'

Renewing my commitment to succeed in growing a successful graphology practice, I created a vision board with photos of everything I wanted to draw into my life—a successful business, money, happy kids, a loving relationship. A year later, I had virtually everything on that board.

Chapter 54

Love at first sight

After getting fired from Bosley Medical Group, and before my handwriting analysis practice took off, my very first temp assignment took me to Ellerbe Becket Architects and Engineers, and Bill McElroy.

It was one of those "love at first sight" things. Even though I worked in that office every day for two weeks without our paths actually crossing, there was that instant spark. When you know, you just know. It wasn't until the last day of my assignment that Bill stopped by the desk I was occupying and asked me to meet him for a drink after work. I asked for a sample of his handwriting. Of course.

Sitting with him in the bar, I shared a few things that his writing revealed: his strong emotions, quick thinking, and love of the "good things in life." My quickie analysis concluded with a statement that proved oh-so-true: "You have a tendency to rush into a new situation, but when it's time for you to make a commitment, you're gone."

Over our twenty-one years of breaking up and getting back together (at least fifty times by my estimate), I learned that while he might be present physically, the emotional commitment was at best equivocal. Life with Bill brought the highest highs and the lowest lows. I could write an entire book about that love/hate story.

We spent hours getting acquainted over white zinfandel—next to Bud Lite, his beverage of choice—and made plans to meet for lunch on Friday at his favorite Mexican cantina. The attraction was undeniable on both sides. Something about him magnetized me, drew me in. However, the three Margaritas he downed at lunch was a red flag that got my attention, but I foolishly chose to ignore.

As I had predicted from his handwriting analysis, Bill was instantly full-on. A picnic on Santa Monica Beach. At dinner at Denim and Diamonds a few nights later, mid-conversation conversation, out of the blue, he said, "I don't know what's going to happen—whether we'll get married and be together for forty years, or—"

"Hold that thought," I interrupted. "It's a little soon to be talking about getting married. We just met."

But that was Bill—all or nothing. For a long time, despite some of the truly awful things he did, he was the love of my life and I'm not always sure why. Some things are just undefinable.

Certainly, his generosity was unlimited. When he was sent to Hawaii to design the electrical and safety systems of the then-new Hawaii Prince Hotel in Waikiki, he took me with him. Twice.

He had a reputation for rushing to pick up the tab anytime we went out with friends. In that first year when I was struggling to eke out a living with handwriting analysis, there was a month that Bill paid my rent.

When he asked what I wanted for my birthday the first year we were together, I said I needed a watch, but don't buy an expensive one, a Timex was fine. He spent $1000 on a Movado Museum Watch which, more than 30 years later, I still wear. Every birthday and Christmas was an occasion for jewelry. Apo, who owned the local jewelry store, joked that he loved to see Bill coming.

After we divorced for the second time, Bill went to England with me and without giving it a second thought, treated my cousins to a thousand-dollar lunch at The Priory, a gorgeous place high on a hill. I sometimes wondered whether the gifts and flowers and meals at good restaurants were meant to be silent apologies for the other times.

The intense love and giddy highs, followed by maddening, raging lows was a metaphor for Jen's and my relationship, too. No wonder she and Bill didn't get along.

At the end of the first year, I wasn't yet making enough money to take the kids to the Beverly Hilton for dinner (not that I wanted to), but we were content going to the local Sizzler Steakhouse and Round Table Pizza once in a while. And I no longer needed temp work.

Chapter 55

21 years of breaking up

When Bill and I started dating in 1989, Jen was seventeen. Four years later we bought a house in Valencia and got married. Erik and Ben, in their mid-teens, lived with us. Jen stayed behind and lived with Nick. Things didn't go well between them, and she frequently called with tales of drugs and scary visitors to the apartment. I subsidized her until she was able to take charge of her life and, to my relief, moved to her own place.

With the exception of their first meeting, when Bill brought Jen a bouquet of pink roses to introduce himself, the two of them barely tolerated each other. Okay, the unlovely truth is, they pretty much hated each other until the last couple years of her life. As if some part of her knew she would be gone soon and she didn't want to leave things unsettled, Jen started reconciling with people, including Bill and me.

When she phoned me and said, "I don't hate you anymore," I took it to mean, "I love you."

The first divorce came in 1998. Before it was final, Bill wanted to get back together, but it was too late and I had moved to an apartment. We remarried in 1999, divorced again in 2004, and stayed together on and off for another six years. I sometimes joke that we spent twenty-one years breaking up, only it really wasn't funny.

For as long as I knew him, Bill lived for the weekend. During the week, he threw himself into work. As a well-regarded electrical engineer, he was responsible for designing the safety systems on major projects that ranged from nuclear power plants to the Jules Stein and Doris Stein Eye Research

Centers at UCLA, to the State and Federal Office buildings downtown, to high rise hotels in Hawaii. He knew how to get things done, even when it meant a little bullying. Contractors referred to him as "Mad Dog McElroy" or "Wild Bill."

In addition to his career as an electrical engineer, he was a pilot of small planes and a flight instructor. He was a nervous passenger, though, as I was surprised to discover when we boarded a plane for a long flight. When he wasn't at the yoke there were few things he enjoyed more than flying the Flight Simulator on his computer. He never drank alcohol before flying. But at all other times, he had a Bud Lite in his hand. He consistently drank three cans an hour, unless he was on the phone to his brother. Then it was five. I counted.

At his best, he was wonderful, warm, affectionate, never said goodbye without an "I love you" and a kiss. He couldn't have been more thoughtful, the kind of partner most women would want. He enjoyed handling mundane chores like taking out the trash, keeping my car washed, making tiny salads for Erik and Ben's guinea pigs. When they were old enough, he bought cars for them both (the boys, not the guinea pigs). Barbecuing on weekends. Flowers virtually every Friday, expensive gifts on birthdays and Christmas. He loved taking me to good restaurants and was super-supportive in many ways.

And then, there was that other side. I used to tease him that he was like the little girl in the poem:

> *There was a little girl, who had a little curl,*
> *Right in the middle of her forehead.*
> *When she was good, she was very, very good.*
> *And when she was bad, she was horrid.*

Or, more to the point, parts of the old Mary Wells song, *Two Lovers:*

He's sweet and kind and he's mine, all mine
He treats me good like a lover should....
Well you know, he treats me bad, makes me sad
Makes me cry, but still I can't deny
That I love him....

That 'split personality' described my relationship with Bill better than anything I could say.

He was a high-functioning alcoholic who was not interested in changing his habits. When I first met him he was a smoker, which shows how strongly I was attracted to him—I couldn't stand the smell of cigarette smoke; was allergic to it. But he only smoked outside and his clothes didn't reek. A year after we started dating, his office went smoke free. The employees were offered group hypnosis to help them dump the habit. Bill was one of those who accepted.

The instructor had everyone tot up how many cigarettes they had smoked over their lifetime. Bill figured his number was around 100,000, and that was enough for him. He quit on the spot. Amazingly, giving up smoking never seemed to bother him, but I couldn't help noticing that his drinking started to increase from three beers a night to infinity. By the time we divorced the second time, he was up to twenty-four a day, and then he started taking gin or vodka to work in a water bottle.

One day when his car was in for repairs, he borrowed mine. He always had a couple of Bud Lite in the "saddlebag" of his car, which he drank on the way to and from work, as well as a twelve-pack in the trunk, but I was more than furious when, backing out of our driveway the next day, and an empty can rolled out from under the driver seat.

"What if I got stopped for some reason and a cop saw that can?" I yelled at him, picturing myself walking that humiliating white line. He was less than contrite.

He liked to say that he drank when he was happy and he drank when he was mad or sad, and he liked it. If I didn't like it, I knew where the door was. His relationship with alcohol played a major role in the end of ours. The good news is, eventually, he quit drinking. The very sad news is, he died of esophageal cancer several years later.

Relationship problems are rarely one-sided, and Bill's complaint about me was the amount of time I spent on my work. "I wouldn't mind if I was last on your list," he was fond of saying angrily, "But I'm not even on your list."

I could make the excuse that I'd had to work long hours to take care of my kids and it had become a habit, but the truth is, I've always been that way, losing myself in my work. On the other hand, sitting on the couch, watching the same reruns every night with someone who is drinking themselves into a stupor is not all that attractive.

And then he would do something really nice. Just like the Mary Wells song—split personality.

Chapter 56

Bill and Lionel

With his engineer's brain, Bill was none too sure about the Afterlife. He was, at least on the surface, open-minded about it enough to put up with all of my ramblings about Spirit.

In the year of Jennifer's death, I talked him into going with me to a seminar being given by Suzanne Northrop, a well-known medium who was speaking at a hotel in Culver City. Her presentation was just before Bill's and my birthdays—they were one day apart—two Scorpios, no wonder we had problems!

During the presentation Suzanne asked, "Who is William?" Reluctantly, at my urging, Bill raised his hand.

She then said, "An older female passed; mother."

He wasn't saying anything, so I said yes.

"She didn't know you, did she?" Suzanne asked me. No. She grinned. "She says he's not always easy." That got a laugh from the audience, including Bill, who had a good sense of humor.

Suzanne's next question: "Who is the person who has trouble with the false teeth?" Bill's father was unable to wear his false teeth at our wedding because they were too painful.

Next, "Who is Tom or Thomas?"

When I said that was the name of the person who killed my daughter, Suzanne said, "Your daughter must have had quite a sense of humor. She's saying 'We took care of him.'"

She went on providing accurate evidence for several minutes. The last thing was, "Who has the Lionel model trains?"

Bill had been laid off from his job and was depressed. I bought him a model train set that he set up on a big table in the garage, and enjoyed spending hours running it. I was sure Suzanne's reference to the trains would have convinced him about Spirit. Instead, when I mentioned it afterwards, he just said, "They're not Lionel."

They might have been a different brand, but Lionel was Suzanne's reference point. When something comes across slightly off like that, it's not because Spirit got it wrong. It's a minor translation issue. Bill just didn't want to be convinced. I thought it was cool, though, that his mom was watching him playing with his train set.

Chapter 57

Spirit finds me a place

B ill and I divorced for the second time in 2004, and yet we continued to be together on and off for another six years. Tired of the constant threat of brushfires in Valencia, I moved forty miles west to Ventura, on the Pacific Coast (yes, ironic, I know).

Finding an apartment proved to be a challenge. I looked around Ventura but wasn't getting anywhere. The places I saw that were affordable weren't very nice, and the expensive ones said I couldn't allow my (Jen's) two cats outside. Fritz and Sugar were indoor-outdoor cats, so that wasn't going to work.

I asked my spirit guides to find me the perfect place at the right price at the right time. A friend referred me to a psychic called AJ Llewellyn, so I booked a reading at her home. as soon as I sat down at her table, Nelson, a big, beautiful, fluffy black cat insisted on jumping up and sitting on the cards she had picked for me.

"He never does that," AJ insisted, trying unsuccessfully to push him off several times. I didn't mine; I was flattered that Nelson wanted to be near me. I love cats of all kinds, as did my daughter. Maybe Jen was whispering in his silky ear.

"You're gonna find an apartment," AJ said, studying the cards she had drawn for me. "There's a view of the ocean." She frowned as if puzzled. "There's something really weird about the carpet. There's a big dark spot on it."

I looked and looked for the right place to rent, but no luck. I'd been driving around for hours one day and was feeling really down and discouraged. Before getting on the freeway and heading back to Valencia, I decided to stop at the Barnes & Noble—books always make me feel better.

As I was driving out of the shopping center, I noticed some nice-looking Cape Cod-style apartments across the street—The Colony, one- and two-bedrooms "Now renting," blared the billboard. Probably too expensive, I guessed, but with nothing to lose, I tapped in the phone number.

"If you can come right now, there's a two-bedroom I can show you," the manager said. "The tenant just moved out. It's the only one I've got."

Five minutes later she was taking me through a well-kept, attractive apartment complex. She unlocked the apartment door and when I walked inside, I couldn't help laughing out loud. In the middle of the carpet was a gigantic black stain. AJ really got that right!

"Oh, don't worry about that," said the manager, not knowing what I found so funny. "The guy who moved out was parking his motorcycle inside. We'll have the carpet cleaned."

As it happened, they thought I was a nice lady, so instead of cleaning the carpet, they ripped it out and put in all new carpeting before the cats and I moved in.

Not only because she was an excellent psychic—she's a warm, generous, compassionate person—AJ and I became fast friends, and remain so today.

Moving to Ventura felt like coming home. Maybe it's because I come from an island—Great Britain—and being close to the ocean reminds me of that. Or maybe because, even with a population of around 120,000, the energy in Ventura was still 'small townish' and virtually everyone you meet is nice. They smile, they wave. They're friendly.

I knew only two people in town. I'd met Raul Melendez (who writes as Peter Sexton), at a mystery writers conference the year Jennifer was killed and I was distracting myself with writing. Raul and I were in a critique group together and became best buds. The other was my friend and writing mentor,

Bob Joseph. It was a lot easier with him living only a couple of miles away to get together and work on my stories.

I tend to be a bit of a hermit, so in order to get out and meet people, I joined the Ventura Chamber of Commerce and became an Ambassador. As a Chamber Ambassador I attended countless ribbon cuttings for business openings, and loads of other public events, including the monthly Chamber Breakfast.

At the Breakfast, members have thirty seconds to introduce themselves and their business. Most members were, like me, sole practitioners looking for clients, but it just so happened that at the first breakfast I attended, someone needed a forensic document examiner.

Handwriting analysis is not something everyone sees a need for, and that was the single client I got from being a Chamber member. But, when my first novel was published, many of those members showed up at my book launch party and bought books. And many of them continue to be my readers and friends who show up. Networking works.

Chapter 58

I jump off a cliff

Over my fifty-plus year career I have analyzed well over ten thousand handwritings, and I was ready to kill someone. On paper, of course. That's when I started writing my Forensic Handwriting suspense series.

My first mystery fiction book, *Poison Pen,* placed third out of 90+ entries in the Southwest Writers competition, but regardless of sending it out to agents and publishers (that's for another memoir), it took seven years of trying before it was published by Capital Crime, a small publisher. The first print run sold out right away. But my nonfiction book, *The Complete Idiot's Guide to Handwriting Analysis* had been published by Macmillan, a major publishing house, and I wanted that for my fiction, too.

A significant part of any success I've had in publishing can be laid at the feet of the Santa Clarita Valley Mystery Writers, a critique group I founded along with Bruce Cook, Gwen Freeman, and Bob Bealmear (AKA Robert Fate). They are better writers than me, and I like to think that some of their talent rubbed off on me over the years we met together. Then I moved to Ventura.

Bill Osgood was a business coach I met at a Chamber of Commerce meeting. He spoke about the first step to success: setting your BHAG—your Big Hairy Audacious Goal. Working with this good-natured, laidback guy and his great ideas, I formulated my BHAG and laid out a plan: have *Poison Pen* published within a year by a major publishing house.

And it happened! The editor at Capital Crimes sent it out to magazines and it got a starred review in *Publishers Weekly* magazine, who called it a "Dynamite debut." I learned that this was a very big deal. Kristen Weber, a senior editor at Obsidian, spotted the review and contacted Capital Crime. Obsidian is a mystery imprint of Penguin, one of the last major publishing houses left in the world. In other words, my dream come true. And there's more—I was being offered a contract for *two* books. I didn't know until that moment that I was writing a series, but that's how *Written in Blood* came about. There is nothing more exciting than receiving a box of your first book in the mail. Except receiving your second book.

Then, I was offered another two-book deal. Woo hoo! I was on my way.

Not.

I had several agents, some with impressive credentials. Like Irene Webb, who represented me in the second Penguin deal. She was responsible for selling *The Godfather* from book to movie. We parted friends when our visions for my career diverged.

While I was writing the fourth book Kristen, who loved the series, left Penguin to get married, and I got orphaned. That's what it's called in publishing when you lose your editor and her successor isn't interested in your work. My new editor seemed intent on sabotaging me, and I didn't get a new contract. But, as "all things work together for good," this led to better things.

Next, I was represented by an agent from another well-known agency. She told me that no publisher would pick up a series in the middle. So I wrote what I thought was a standalone book called *What She Saw*, a story about a girl with amnesia, where my series characters played a smaller but important role. For whatever reason, she didn't sell the book, and then I moved to Suspense Publishing, a smaller but excellent house local to me.

We got my rights back from Penguin and Suspense repackaged the first four books, plus *What She Saw*, and they published my next several books. We were geographically close enough to go out to lunch once in a while, and the owners, John and Shannon Raab, came to my book launches. They are good people and I love them to bits. But...

The pandemic hit and we all know about that. It hit my publisher hard and at the end of 2021, I reviewed my sales numbers in dismay. It wasn't their fault they got Covid and were not able to promote my books in the way they needed promoting. With fewer days ahead of me than are behind me, something drastic needed to happen, and feeling the hot breath of time on my neck, I couldn't afford to let my books languish and wait for readers to find them.

Victoria, a fellow member of a group called the Blackbird Writers, who support each other in all ways other writers can, was successfully promoting her husband's mysteries. She volunteered to help me with advertising, which seemed to be the way forward. And that meant publishing my work independent of a traditional publisher.

I had just completed the manuscript for *Dead Letters,* the eighth title in my Claudia Rose series, and it was set for release by Suspense in August. I hated having to make the split, and they were not happy with my decision to leave the 'family.' But if I was to meet my next publishing goals—my new BHAG—it was a difficult step that needed to be taken.

After asking my spirit guides whether I was making the right decision, I emailed my author friend, Peg Brantley, and told her what I'd done. The subject line read: *I just jumped off a cliff.* I clicked Send and went to buy groceries.

Driving across town to WinCo, I was listening to NPR's Fresh Air. Terry Gross was interviewing Sir Patrick Stewart of Star Trek fame. He was speaking about an early mentor in his acting career, who, he said, had told him, "You have to take risks. You have to be brave. *You have to step into the unknown.*"

Wow! I thought. My guides were answering my question. That had to be a direct message for me. And then, Sir Patrick continued, *"You have to step off the edge of a cliff."*

What?! Did he really just say that? It's exactly what I wrote to Peg. How clear could the message be? But he wasn't done yet. He finished with this: "I always make sure I'm **dead letter** perfect."

I burst into tears of gratitude. The book I'd just written was titled *Dead Letters*!!! I had made the right choice (that's a play on my business name of thirty years: Sheila Lowe & Associates, *The Write Choice!)* I founded a new imprint just for my own books and called it Write Choice Ink.

A year later, I'm a lot closer to where I wanted to be than I was when I started. It's been an expensive learning curve, getting new covers for all the books and rebranding them again, twice. I worked with a top-notch marketing group in Italy for a while, and am now relying on Valerie Biel, another Blackbird writer who is an incredible expert in Facebook and Amazon advertising. Finally, the needle is moving in the right direction.

Chapter 59

The media and me

My YouTube channel is a journey through my adult life, from the slimmer, dark-haired me to the *zaftig* (Yiddish for 'full-figured') version with long, (all natural) platinum-colored hair.

I uploaded some of the many TV interviews I've given over the years, from small, local shows, to national, and even international ones. Several episodes from the 90s are from when I was the handwriting analyst for the *Hard Copy* show. In one segment, I talked about OJ Simpson's suicide letter. In another, the signature on the will of Nicole Brown Simpson was being questioned. One episode concerned Susan Smith, a young mother who drowned her children by sending her car into a lake with them in it. For weeks she blamed an unknown Black man. Finally, she handwrote a two-page confession.

One of my shortest court appearances that ended up on TV was in the murder case of the so-called 'Clark Rockefeller.' I testified on camera for all of ten minutes.

A German national whose real name was Christian Karl Gerthartsreiter, "Rockefeller" had been in the news for kidnapping his little daughter. In a carefully orchestrated stunt, he had grabbed her off the street from a social worker who was supervising their visit.

While he was being investigated for the kidnapping, police discovered that Gerhartsreiter was a person of interest in the San Marino, California disappearance of a young couple, Jon and Linda Sohus in the 1980s. Eight years after they disappeared, male human remains were uncovered in the garden of the home where the couple had lived. Gerhartsreiter, also known as Christopher Chichester and other aliases, had lived in the guesthouse. Evidence pointed to him as Jon Sohus' killer. No sign of Linda was ever found.

At least one movie was made about the case, and I had been contacted by a reporter at the *Pasadena Star* newspaper to examine two postcards sent to friends and relatives of Linda Sohus. The question was: did Linda write them, or did Gerhartsreiter? Several of my colleagues had already opined that the handwriting was not Linda's. At first, I agreed. But after examining additional writing samples that I requested, my initial opinion changed. I've given lectures and appeared (very briefly) on Dateline NBC, explaining my strong opinion that Linda wrote the postcards.

A grand jury was convened in Los Angeles County and the materials I had used were subpoenaed (though nobody ever paid me for the work), along with my report. I was never called to testify before that grand jury, but when Gerhartsreiter was extradited from Boston and put on trial, his attorney, Brad Bailey, called to say that he wanted to retain me to testify in the case.

"I don't want to testify for your client," I replied. "I believe he's probably guilty."

Mr. Bailey assured me that all he wanted was for me to tell the truth about my opinion. Their theory of the case was that Linda Sohus had killed her husband and fled to Europe—the postcards were postmarked in France—despite the fact that Linda had never had a passport, and the marriage was a happy one.

I took the witness stand with the big fish eye lens of a TV camera facing me from the back of the courtroom. The accused murderer, a small, unprepossessing man seated at the defense table, never looked at me. He had managed to con a lot of people, and was very likely a killer.

Brad Bailey asked me only a couple of questions, and didn't give me the opportunity to present demonstrative evidence of my opinion, as is usual. Then it was the Assistant District Attorney's turn. His cross-examination was even more brief.

"Ms. Lowe, you believe the handwriting on the postcards was done by Linda Sohus?"

"Yes."

"Do you know the circumstances under which they were written?"

"No." In fact, I was thinking, Gerhartsreiter could well have been holding a gun to Linda's head.

"That's all for this witness," said the ADA.

"The witness may be excused," said the judge, and I stepped down.

After I testified, I learned that, like me, Linda Sohus' family and friends believed the handwriting on the postcards to be hers. Not only that, but the document examiner who testified for L.A. County agreed.

Another high-profile case was the Jon Benet Ramsey ransom note. The Denver Post sent me copies of all the documents that had been examined in that apparently shoddy investigation. There is a specific method for taking handwriting exemplars and the police on the case did not follow it. I know this because I was a founding member of a committee that authored the guidelines for how to do it.

From my point of view as a document examiner, assuming the reporting was correct, the most egregious mistake the police made was allowing the parents, John and Patsy Ramsey, to prepare their comparison exemplars in their own time. Dictation of the material that is in question should be given at varying speeds and written with each hand.

Only one brief paragraph was submitted that was written by John Ramsey. It was not dictated from the three-page ransom letter as it should have been, and as Patsy Ramsey had submitted.

Once again, several document examiners had opined that Patsy wrote the three-page ransom note. My respected Italian colleague, Fausto Brugnatelli, agreed with me that based upon what we examined, she probably had not. Additionally, based on that small sample of his handwriting, we failed to understand why John Ramsey was ruled out as the writer.

Rolanda, a TV talk show invited me to appear on a panel that included Robert Ressler, the FBI agent who founded the Bureau's Behavioral Profiling Unit. They flew me to New York on the red eye. There were about six passengers in that big plane, which may be why, for once, I didn't experience my usual white-knuckle fear of flying.

After a $24 bagel and tea with my close friend and mentor, Roger Rubin, who lived in Manhattan, there were a few hours to rest in a boutique hotel on Central Park. The show people sent a car for the evening taping, and I sat in the greenroom for a couple of hours, chatting with Robert Ressler.

He had been to the Ramsey home in Boulder, Colorado and was firmly of the opinion that the child's father was the most likely person responsible for her death. As soon as the show was over, I headed straight to the airport. My trip to New York and back lasted a total of twenty-seven hours.

A few days after the 1994 harrowing Northridge earthquake I was scheduled to appear on the *KTLA Morning Show.* They wanted to talk about the handwriting of the hosts, and Elvis, and Bill Clinton. An overpass had fallen onto the freeway in the quake, killing a highway patrol officer, and making travel virtually impossible. So, rather than spending six hours on an alternate road to get to the studio, I went via Metrolink, which meant traveling through a mountain to get to the Los Angeles studio. Southern California was experiencing literally thousands of aftershocks that week. There was a collective sigh of relief when the train exited the tunnel.

Another show, *Unscripted with Chris Connelly,* used to send a town car to pick me up in Valencia and drive me to Disneyland, where they taped the

ESPN show at a restaurant on the outer edge of the Park. Chris would show me a screen that displayed an array of sports figures' signatures and ask me to comment on their personalities.

There are several shows for which I've done tapings that as far as I know still haven't aired—one for Fox called *The Criminal Mind*, where I was part of a panel, talking about what happened to my daughter. One of the panelists was a well-known TV medium. Another show that's possibly to air in summer of 2023 is The Jennifer Pandos Story, a documentary about a young woman who went missing in the late 1980s and was never found. In her room, her mother found a strange handwritten note. My task was to give an opinion on who wrote it.

Through the years I have done hundreds of radio, magazine, newspaper, and blog interviews worldwide about people in the news—Tiger Woods, Princess Diana, Prince Harry and Meghan Markle, baseball players, country and western singers—you'd think I would be famous by now.

Few of these venues pay for an interview or appearance. They sell it this way: *Think of the free publicity you'll get!* Knowing better, I just laugh and say, Okay.

Some of these appearances on my YouTube channel. The ones that dealt with Jennifer's murder are there, too.

Chapter 60

Tom comes through

Especially in recent years, my daughter's killer, Tom Schnaible, has come through in several readings, wanting to apologize for what he did to Jennifer. A wonderful medium, Tracey Bolton, said she had tears welling up as he spoke to her. "He says 'you were one of the only people who had insight into me.'"

"Your attempts to understand him, and the sense of maternal caring for him, enabled him to get some healing on the Other Side."

"He is not making excuses; nobody deserved what he did," Tracey said. "There was mental confusion, like he wasn't inside his body and is horrified at his action. He now sees the ripple effect of his action."

Tom began showing up at every reading I had, continuing to apologize. He never asked for forgiveness, but I told him that I sincerely forgave him and that he no longer needed to come.

Not everyone understands how I could forgive the man who brutally murdered my daughter. I have never hated him. Despite deploring what he did, and grieving deeply for Jennifer, I have never hated him.

Besides, you know what they say about hating someone—it's like drinking poison and expecting the other person to die.

Chapter 61

Psychic junkie

From my very first reading I became a psychic junkie. But after Jennifer crossed over to the Other Side, I started going specifically to mediums. What's the difference? Simply that all mediums are psychic, but not all psychics are mediums. Some of the mediums I've worked with were astonishing in the evidence they brought through. A few were really bad. Others may have been good but I just didn't relate to them.

One famous person charged $250 and insisted on talking about my relationship with my mother, who was (and as I write this still is) alive. I explained that I had resolved my issues with my mother and didn't want to spend my time or money talking about them. As the medium refused to leave the subject alone, I began to suspect that it was her own issues with her own mother that were behind her insistence to stay on it.

No medium is 100% correct, just like no handwriting analyst is. But any errors are made on this side of the veil. Think of it as being like someone translating English to Chinese or vice versa. Some words or idioms aren't going to come across exactly as they were intended. Spirit wasn't wrong; it's the medium (the translator) who missed some subtlety.

In the following pages, I will be sharing in some detail a few of my experiences with mediums who have brought comfort and healing to many, including me.

Chapter 62
Chris Meredith

Reverend Chris Meredith from Cheshire, England has a wicked sense of humor. When I first knew him he was conducting mediumship sessions in his home at the Harmony Grove Spiritualist Association. It was a lovely little community in the woods in Escondido.

My first session was three years after Jennifer's transition to spirit. As always when I visit a medium for the first time I had told him nothing about me or my reason for being there. He turned on the tape recorder and sat quietly as he moved into a trance. His voice changed a little—a bit more posh.

The first part of the reading was about several of my family members. Eventually Jen came through.

"Are you here to connect with a person who died under traumatic circumstances?" Chris asked. "This was a younger person, coming into the prime of life. Another party brought about the death. Was it your child? A girl?"

I just said yes. "She says it wasn't your fault," He continued. "There's a wonderful light within her soul as her energy is beginning to change. She wants you to know she's okay...It happened very suddenly. She had an impact to her head."

Chris talked about my Uncle John and how he was there to meet her when she arrived on the Other Side.

"She's dealing with the emotional impact of what happened. She was here one minute, and standing by her body the next."

Jennifer also talked about Tom. "We banged heads. I was very strong-willed and stubborn. I lived my life to the full and did what I wanted to do. I wouldn't change it...I know the relationship was dysfunctional. He will pay the price."

Several of my mother's family came through—Uncle Roy, my mother's cousin Jack. My grandmother (who often makes herself known). Chris said, "She's quite a lass." He even got her name, which is not common: Elsie.

As a couple of other mediums have told me, Chris also said that Jennifer was getting more involved with music as a healing tool, and she is working with children who were also killed dramatically.

He talked about my books, too, and Penguin publishing my writing (which they later did).

In 2010 I drove down to Harmony Grove for a reading. I handed Chris a brand new sealed-in-the package cassette tape and watched him open it just as my session began. On my way home I put the tape in the cassette player in my car (I have an old car). As it started to play, I nearly shot through the roof. I'm quite sure the hair stood up on my neck.

Just before Chris' voice began to speak, there was a very short sound that was distinctly not human. It sounded like a loud whisper, long and drawn out: "I—think." That had never happened before nor did it happen again. When I got home, I found someone who worked with EVP (electronic voice phenomena) and emailed her the sound. She sped it up and sent it back to me. Now, it sounds like "Mommy!" So, I don't know what to make of that.

Years later, after hearing a talk by Sheri Perl, who has made an in-depth study in EVP, I tried it for myself, but was not very successful. Still, that one personal experience was good enough for me.

I had nearly a dozen readings at Chris' home in the century-old Harmony Grove. Sadly, in 2014, his house and twenty-five others were destroyed in the Cocos fire. He was given ten minutes to collect his dogs and make a run for it. He found a new home in Oceanside, but I twisted his arm to start giving sessions over Zoom. It's a lot easier than making that long drive.

Chapter 63

Adventures in online dating

I had always scorned online dating. That's how Bill met several women, including the one he married after me. I knew this because after the second divorce—we were gluttons for punishment, continuing to see each other—he was using my laptop when he came to stay for the weekend and left it open on the eHarmony website.

Sometimes you do things you never intended to.

I was on the phone, listening to a friend telling me about someone she knew who had found true love through OkCupid. As she spoke I idly keyed in the URL for the dating site and without consciously thinking about what I was doing, filled out the profile information.

I looked over the potential matches the site offered and was attracted to a guy in the very first photo that popped up. He was dressed casually in a sweatshirt and loose trousers with chunky sandals, sitting on the steps of a temple in India. Wiry hair sprouted untamed all over his head (think 'Albert Einstein'). Although he didn't look best pleased to be photographed, and it wasn't quite a smile that stretched his mouth, there was something engaging in his gaze.

I read his profile, the things he liked to do: international travel, ride around Ventura on his bicycle, shop at garage sales. Nope. Nope. And nope. None of that interested me. I'm a boring person who has few interests outside of working and reading. So, I shrugged and looked at some of the other profiles that were supposedly a match for me.

That summer I went on dates with nine different men, some of them moderately interesting, some barely tolerable. I found the process excruciating. Besides the fact that I hadn't dated since meeting Bill in 1989, it felt unnatural.

Larry, the first guy I met, was a videographer. We had a pleasant chat over Italian food at Cafe Fiore, but we both knew there were no sparks flying. He told me about his adventures at the Burning Man Festival, and I told him about my career in handwriting. A small something did come out of that date. Larry videotaped a lecture I gave on relationship compatibility, the idea being for me to sell copies of the DVD and split the proceeds. Sadly, that never brought either of us within a thousand miles of riches.

Most of the dates were so unmemorable that I've forgotten them.

Marvin, date number eight, could have been something more if I hadn't embarrassed him. We met for coffee at Starbucks and hit it off. After a long chat, he phoned the same day and asked If I would like to see *The Great Gatsby* at the local cheap theater. Why, yes, I would.

I didn't like the movie, but afterwards we continued our conversation for a couple more hours at my house. I was interested enough to have seen him again, but when he was leaving, he leaned in to kiss me. I know it's old school, but I'd like to know somebody for more than a day before swapping spit with them. I turned my head and his lips caught my cheek. That was the last I heard from Marvin.

The last one before I gave up online dating was a guy whose avatar was "Dick the Sailor." He was well-named, and not because he sailed his multi-million-dollar sailboat around the world.

We arranged to meet at Paradise Cove Beach Café in Malibu, where parking was an insane $40. That's typical Malibu, where more celebrities live than any other stretch of land in the world. Dick did not match his profile photo, and within five minutes of our meeting, all I wanted was to end the date and hightail it home. Alone.

While waiting for our table on the sand, we took a short walk. The first thing Dick wanted to know was, "What do you think about sex?"

The appropriate response would have been, "It's great; just not with you." But after driving all that way I stayed for dinner. Luckily, the evening wasn't a total waste—the pecan crusted halibut was delicious.

Afterwards Dick walked me to my car and returned to his original asininity.

"I look forward to exploring the cleavage," he said. OMG! Seriously? I was wearing jeans and a sleeveless tee with an open camp shirt over the top. Nothing remotely sexy.

I phoned him on my way home and said it wasn't going to work out. I took the blame, explaining that with my work schedule I wasn't a good relationship risk. He expressed disappointment at not getting to "explore the cleavage." What a complete jerk.

That's when I decided online dating was not for me. And then, guess what happened.

Chapter 64

It was that guy...

The guy who had first caught my attention—the one who liked all those activities that didn't interest me—messaged me. His name was Arnie. We messaged back and forth a few times, and then he asked if he could call me.

Voices are important, and I liked his a lot. It was, well, rich. When I asked his surname he said, "Richman. I am always a rich man." Corny, but not too.

"Tell me something about yourself," I said.

He answered without hesitation. "I'm cheap."

I am in no way materialistic—if I was, I'd be wealthy—but generosity is a state of being. I had been married to a stingy man and a generous man. Except for Bill's alcoholism, generous was way better. Still, neither of those husbands had worked out well for me. Maybe I needed to branch out and try something new.

It wasn't a shortage of funds that made him cheap; he simply loved nothing more than to find a bargain and then squeeze it to a mushy pulp. When we ate out there was virtually always a coupon involved. When I cooked for him, though, he contributed groceries and helped with the cooking and cleaning up.

We met for the first time at Two Trees Cafe in my neighborhood. I ordered a Diet Coke, Arnie drank water. And we sat there talking for at least two hours. When we finally said goodbye, I went to the nearby grocery store, which shared a parking lot with Two Trees. Guess who followed me over there. And wanted to get together again that evening. We were hooked on each other.

Arnie was a Capricorn (like my dad), born to Jewish parents, though not religious (like my dad), so there was something vaguely familiar. He was not my type, nor I his, but he made me laugh. All the time. And that was so very appealing.

On Fridays we frequented Yolanda's Mexican restaurant. For the price of a beer—neither of us drank more than one—Arnie could make a dinner of their free hors d'oeuvres. On summer Sundays we would go downtown Ventura for pizza and a beer at Café Fiore, where we danced to Reggae music. We were no Fred Astaire and Ginger Rogers, but we had a good time.

I didn't go to garage sales with him, but his shopping jaunts paid off for me. He was forever bringing me gifts worth having. Brand new kitchen accessories picked up for a song. A Toby jug teapot, an Isis brooch. I treasure the beautifully decorated wooden box that he knew was perfect to store many of the essential oils I used.

And then there was Scrabble. We played a game or two, sometimes three, nearly every time we were together. He was really good at the game and I was not. Once he had taught me his strategies we were more evenly matched. Whenever I won, he would jokingly accuse me of cheating.

But...as in every relationship, there were issues. Ours came in the form of a woman named Maureen. They'd been together in the past and she wanted the relationship to continue, while he didn't. He warned me about her the very first time we met—a red flag I should have paid attention to. You may have noticed by now, I've had a bad habit of ignoring those red flags, even when I knew better.

Long before I knew him Arnie had been hospitalized with a staph infection and nearly died (a possible exit point?). Because Maureen had helped him while he was ill, he felt obligated to stay friends with her. She had also tragically lost an adult son to an aneurysm two years earlier—a loss she could not begin to deal with—and Arnie wanted to support her.

Several times a week they went to the gym and out to lunch, and early on weekends to garage sales. Since I didn't want to go to the gym or get up early for garage sales, I couldn't very well complain. But I didn't like it at all.

Maureen became a problem, often phoning his land line at the most inconvenient moments. We could hear her plaintive voice whining loudly as the answering machine picked up: "Arnie, why are you doing this to me? You know how much you're hurting me. Are you with Sheila right now?" And so on. And, as was my bad habit, I put up with it.

⸘

Arnie had a hard time expressing physical affection. I had to teach him what I had learned from Bill—to say goodbye with a kiss. Arnie's and my childhoods had left both of us poorly equipped in that area. Ironically, Bill was very affectionate and liked holding hands in public. One of his great qualities was invariably waking up with a smile.

Ben was getting married and I was flying to Germany for the wedding. Arnie gave me a ride to the airport shuttle, saw me onboard, said goodbye, and stepped down from the bus. Suddenly, he wheeled around and got back on board and shocked me with a proper kiss goodbye. In front of everyone! From him, this said more than a thousand words.

Our relationship continued for more than two years. He sometimes talked about getting married, or moving in with me, but that could never happen. I'm no neat freak, but his place was a mess. We alternated visiting at each other's homes, only seven miles apart, with a promise that the relationship was a committed one.

And then I discovered in exactly the same way I had found Bill was cheating, that Arnie was still communicating with other women through dating sites. He had accessed his email on my computer while I was sitting next to him at my desk. When I saw the long list of emails between him and these women, I asked, "What the hell?"

He knew instantly that he had made a fatal error. His claim that it was "just a game," and "meant nothing," didn't pass the smell test. Did those women know it was a game? I demanded. What if he wanted to meet one of them? He claimed he never had met with any of them, but how could I trust that? I felt utterly betrayed.

I cared about him too much to give him up as a friend, but out of self-respect, told we could no longer be anything more. He clearly regretted it, but there was nothing he could do to console me. I wasn't about to give him a chance to hurt me like that again. I was making the choice, but I couldn't stop weeping.

Psychologists tell us that when we are deeply upset about something, it may be due, not to the present situation, but to pain from the past being re-experienced on an unconscious level. With Arnie's behavior, and with Bill's, I was going through another form of the abandonment I had experienced from my both of my parents—my dad leaving us to start another family, and my mother shunning me because of her religion.

Chapter 65

Arnie's exit point

Arnie and I continued to see each other as friends. We continued to play Scrabble, went to concerts in the park; had meals together. One night near the end of November I could see something was troubling him and asked what was up.

He hesitated for a long time then said, "I was lying in bed last night, thinking that I'm going to die."

"You'd better not," I warned, only half-kidding. "If you die, I'll be mad at you."

A few weeks earlier, we had been playing Scrabble when Arnie started having slight chest pains. Oddly, a few minutes later, my elderly neighbor asked me to call 911 because she, too, was having chest pains. We went and sat with her, waiting for the paramedics. After they checked her out, Arnie asked them to check him, too. They did, and suggested he go to the hospital. He opted not to.

This was a man who complained every single day of being tired and of 'not feeling great.' He had been treated for a tumor on the parathyroid, which was cured, but his doctors could never find anything else wrong, despite his many visits.

Sunday, December 3rd, 2016, a week after telling me he was going to die, Arnie called and said he didn't feel good and was coming over. Being used to hearing it, I didn't take it too seriously and was privately a little peeved—I was preparing for a trial coming up on Tuesday and needed to focus. He said he didn't want to be alone and promised not to interfere with my work. Of course I wasn't going to refuse.

He had been riding his bike at the beach when he began experiencing chest pains again. A paramedic friend of his lived near where he was riding, and Arnie stopped there to rest. After taking his vitals, his friend offered him a ride to the hospital. Once again, Arnie gave that idea a thumbs down. They loaded his bike in the friend's truck and the friend drove him home.

It was mid-afternoon when he drove his Prius to my house, again refusing all offers to take him to the emergency room. "I don't want to sit for hours, waiting to be seen," he said. The chest pains had stopped, but he didn't feel like eating, which was unusual. Now it was his stomach hurting, and he commented that he kept needing to pee. I didn't know then that this was a sign of an impending heart attack—the body trying to rid itself of excess salt.

I had trained and worked as a reflexologist in the 1970s. I gave him a foot treatment, which helped settle him, and I suggested he lie down and rest. He wanted me to stay with him, which I did, still not recognizing that anything more serious than usual was wrong. Whatever else was going on, his sense of humor was intact. He pretended to try and seduce me, joking that if I fell for it, it would probably kill him.

At 1:15 a.m., he told me he had forgotten his wallet and was going home. If he ended up going to the hospital he would need his insurance card. I called fifteen minutes later to make sure he'd arrived safely.

"Did you think I wouldn't make it?" he joked, making fun of my checking up on him. "I'm going to call the twenty-four-hour nurse, and I'll talk to you in the morning."

Around 5:30 the next morning, his son, Matthew, called and woke me up. "I'm at the hospital," he said. "We lost my dad in the night."

Chapter 66

Grieving again

Every death, every grief is different. It was only after losing Arnie that I came to realize just how connected we had been. I grieved him in a way that I had never grieved before. In the past when I had lost someone close to me, I pushed away the anguish and distracted myself by working. This time, I allowed myself to fully experience the feelings in the moment, and it was wretched.

I couldn't stop crying, couldn't stop thinking about him, talking about him, missing his larger-than-life physical presence. There was a heaviness in the air I breathed.

His son, Matthew, told me that after Arnie spoke to me at 1:30 a.m., he had driven himself to Community Memorial Hospital, a mile and a half from where he lived. He had always expressed a deep antipathy for that hospital, which is where he had nearly died ten years earlier. For him to go there tells me that he had to have been really afraid.

He checked himself into the ER and was taken to an examining room, where he was left alone, waiting for someone to give him tests. Ten minutes later he was heard to cry out. He had collapsed, and though medical personnel apparently worked on him for forty-five minutes, they were unable to revive him. He was sixty-eight.

A memorial service would be held at a later date, when his daughter, Abra, could get here from out of state. Meanwhile, Matthew was kind enough to invite me, along with a couple of Arnie's close friends, to view his remains before he was cremated. It took all the guts I could gather to walk up the chapel aisle to the open casket. It reminded me of seeing Jennifer, who had looked like somebody else. The man who lay there didn't look quite the same as the one I had known and loved despite the reasons why I shouldn't.

I had put the best Scrabble tiles—Q, Z, J, X, K—in a little cloth bag, and left it with him.

Chapter 67

Arnie, loud and clear

Of all the highly accomplished evidential mediums I have met, Robert Brown is perhaps the most impressive. A year or two after Jennifer crossed over, he was visiting the US and in the session I booked, made a remarkable connection with her.

From time-to-time Robert would send out email newsletters. Seventeen years after my session, and a month after Arnie's transition to spirit, an email from his office in England offered a discounted rate for a phone session. Mind you, the discount was $300/hour instead of $500, and some of the best mediums I've sat with have charged less than half that amount. But that earlier session was so good, I bit the bullet and made the appointment. It was well worth the expense.

When I called Robert he had no idea that he had worked with me all those years ago. Nor did he know of my current situation. The session started this way:

"A gentleman is rubbing your back, comforting. There was a heart condition. Not a lot of hugging and kissing." From spirit, Arnie told Robert that he felt he hadn't expressed enough of what I meant to him and had been trying to show me he was okay.

He'd always made me laugh, and he continued to even from beyond the veil.

Despite his reluctance—or more accurately inability—to use affectionate terms or say "I love you," there were times when, mocking himself, he would facetiously call me 'cupcake,' or 'pumpkin.' Now, Robert said Arnie was telling me, "You were my prize, my cupcake, apple, cherry pie." For any skeptics in the group, that's not something a medium could make up, and nobody besides me knew this.

If I'd had any doubts about who was coming through (I didn't), the next thing Robert said would have swept them aside.

"I thought I would impress her with my hair."

That crazy, uncontrollable Einstein hair! I really laughed at that.

The next thing he said was that it was a quick passing. "I was such a fool. I could have, should have—"

He also mentioned "good photos of me," and that he "liked the one in the frame." Early in our relationship, shrugging off his dislike of being photographed, I had taken a couple of really good pictures of him. I gave them to Matthew, who enlarged and framed the best one for his memorial.

I was taking notes at the speed of light while Robert talked fast and nonstop for the entire hour we were on the phone.

He said Arnie wanted me to know that there was no point in my going to the hospital; there was nothing I could have done. This meant more to me than I can adequately express. When he decided to go home that last night, I didn't bother to get out of bed, just said goodbye and let him see himself out. I deeply regretted that, and carried a bit of guilt. When Matthew told me, "We don't blame you," I had the feeling that what he was really saying was, "We blame you."

Robert said that Arnie had met up with my daughter and recognized her from what I had told him about her. She had been teaching him how to communicate through a medium so he could talk to me. Jennifer has a lot of young kids around her, Robert relayed, and is acting as a teacher. This was something I'd heard before from other mediums, so it was a meaningful confirmation.

There was much more—an hour packed full of accurate and amazing information, some highly personal, and most of which I could verify. It was so, so comforting.

After Arnie crossed over, several of the readings I got were consistent in him expressing regret that he hadn't treated me better. Another outstanding British medium, Reverend Chris Meredith, talked about the comfortable connection we had, and my patience with him, which again made me laugh. Arnie often said, "You're a very patient woman."

He hoped I would forgive his shortcomings. "I'm amazed she stuck with me," Arnie said to Chris. Numerous times he said to me, "What are you doing with a f**kup like me?"

There was so much of him coming through in this reading: that he felt safe with me and yet, his difficulty with commitment. He talked about the problem he had in prioritizing, which we joked about all the time—how hard it was for him to make a choice and stick with it.

Him saying "I do miss the cooking" was deeply significant. We enjoyed preparing meals together and cleaning up together.

"He had a big heart," Chris said. It was a beautiful, soft heart.

Arnie attended his memorial, and told Chris that he appreciated the way people came together and told stories about him. He was impressed with the simplicity and lack of structure of the event—it truly represented who he was. His son had deliberately made it unstructured, and Arnie would have been the first in line at the taco truck Matthew had behind the venue.

His crazy hair came up yet again.

"I feel like I need to pat down my hair," Chris said. "It's like I was dragged through a hedge backwards. "Arnie says, 'it's still the same.'"

"Humor was his saving grace."

His ability to make me laugh all the time was, for me, one of his most endearing qualities.

Arnie's friend Maureen died about three months after him (she had been out of the country when he died, and was not able to attend the memorial). She was found alone in her condo. I think it's likely that that between losing her son, and then Arnie, she probably died of a broken heart. I can't in all honesty say I was pleased that she followed him across the veil, but in later readings was told that they were not together on the same plane of existence.

Despite the fact that when Arnie crossed I had been trying to break off the relationship, I was having a very hard time losing him. Having our loved ones come through in a mediumship session—knowing they are still alive, even if we can't see them with our eyes—is a great comfort. But it cannot replace their physical presence.

Sometimes the people we love come to visit in vivid dreams. About six months after Arnie crossed over, I had such a visit. He looked a lot younger, and despite being Caucasian, wore his hair in a big Afro—dark, not salt-and-pepper, as I'd last seen him. More than once he had described wearing his hair this way in his youth, and how, when traveling to Turkey, he had nearly ended up in jail for smoking pot. I knew instantly that it was him.

In the dream, he said, "I need to let you know that I'm not going to be around all the time anymore. But I'll be back to visit."

When I woke up in the morning, something felt different, lighter. I knew his spirit was no longer there with me. After that, I was able to start moving forward again.

Chapter 68

There is no death

Somewhere, somehow, I learned about AREI: Afterlife Research and Education Institute, and their weekend symposium in Scottsdale, Arizona.

One of around five hundred attendees—a lot of people are interested in learning about the Afterlife—I attended presentations given by several people who have since become friends and mentors.

Suzanne Giesemann started out as a left-brained Naval Commander. The lightning-strike death of her pregnant stepdaughter led her to investigate what happens when the body dies. Her explorations have resulted in her becoming one of the best-recognized mediums in the field. When my book, *Proof of Life*, was released, she gave me a beautiful cover blurb. Suzanne also brought Jennifer through in mediumship session that was filled with accurate evidence. In return, I analyzed Suzanne's handwriting and appeared as a guest on her then-radio show, *Messages of Hope*.

It was a great privilege to meet Wendy Zammit from Australia. She and her husband, Victor, a retired lawyer, have a website with more information about the Afterlife community and resources than just about anyone else. Along with Karyn Jarvie, another friend I met at AREI, Wendy hosts a free weekly Zoom meeting called the Global Gathering. For information about attending: www.victorzammit.com

Sheri Perl and her husband played off each other like Stiller & Meara comedy duo, but they spoke about a serious subject: EVP (electronic voice phenomena). Using messages she has gotten from her son on the Other Side, Sheri demonstrated how anyone can record these voices. She hosts the Prayer

Registry website, which gives parents a place to honor their children who have crossed over. https://www.sheriperl.com/the-prayer-registry

The year after Jennifer's transition I had attended a seminar in Arizona hosted by Gary Schwartz, Ph.D.. At his lab at the U of A, he triple-blind tested some of the best-known mediums in the US. The remarkable results provided a scientific basis for evidence that life goes on beyond earth. For the past several years, Gary has been working on the 'Soul Phone,' a device intended to make it easy for everyone to communicate with the Other Side.

Another pair of scientific researchers I met were Michelle Szabo, RTM and Dennis Grega, Ph.D. Their *Voices Across the Veil,* books a small group of up to six participants who, for a nominal fee ($40 each as of this writing) receive a brief online reading from a tested medium. To help Dennis and Michelle collect data for their research, attendees complete a questionnaire before and after the session. https://voicesacrosstheveil.afterlifedata.com/

Mark Anthony, "the psychic lawyer," had a made for TV personality and appearance. His easy way of relating to people made everyone want to book a reading with him.

Perhaps the most stunning session I attended was with Brazilian scientist and medium, Sonia Rinaldi, whose work has been guided by scientists on the Other Side. Scientists like Nikola Tesla, who explained that he works at what is called the North Station. Sonia started over more than thirty years ago with EVP, and has progressed to bringing through impressive color images of people in spirit, as well as animals and ETs.

When it comes to spiritual things, I am a skeptic until I see proof. The many images Sonia shared in her presentation convinced me, especially since the techniques she uses can be easily reproduced by anyone with a smartphone. To see how she does it, you are invited to view the recording of her last visit to the Zoom group I host. https://youtu.be/PQVCYsvDC

I was lucky enough to become part of Sonia's "Group of 30 moms." The spirit people who participate in the experiment have to remember what they looked like here and try to reconstruct that as closely as they can. Often, if they crossed when they were in older age they show themselves younger. And, some who were very young, show themselves older. The images of Jennifer are clearly her, but, twenty-three years later—not exactly as she was on earth.

Later, Sonia allowed me to join another of her projects when she was bringing through males. I sent her a photo of Bill to help him come through. What came back was undeniably him, only younger, and nothing like the photo I had sent her. On top of that, Sonia received, as she often does, images of unidentified spirit people who came through. One of them in this batch is, I believe, Arnie.

There was another Symposium the next year. I flew back to Scottsdale and was one of eight-hundred people in attendance.

Scott Milligan, a medium from England, went into a trance state and answered questions from the audience through his spirit communicator. This was so far from my JW upbringing that I might have been on another planet. I loved it.

There was a class in scrying with a black mirror, which is akin to looking into a crystal ball. These are ways to focus attention and get messages from spirit. I can't say I've ever been successful with it, but the blame is fully on my lack of focus.

At the end of the symposium, Craig Hogan, PhD. and our host, gathered everyone in the main ballroom and talked about his plan to form Zoom groups around the world to discuss specific spiritual topics. This was before Covid and the popularity of Zoom, but I was very familiar with the platform, having used it with my handwriting analysis organization since 2013.

Craig asked what topics people would like these groups to cover. Some said physical mediumship, some wanted spirit drawings, others asked for development circles. Automatic writing seemed like a natural for a handwriting analyst, so I raised my hand and made that suggestion. My intention was to join a group led by a good teacher and learn how to do automatic writing myself. What happened was, I suddenly found myself appointed as a group leader.

Five interested people showed up for the first meeting. We got acquainted and I explained that I was not going to be their teacher, but was simply there as a facilitator for the discussion. I'd found several good articles to share about how to prepare for automatic writing. By the end of the hour-long meeting, we had set the intention to practice daily and report back on what happened (or didn't happen) next time.

Automatic writing, it turns out, can be a number of things, including typing on a keyboard, taking dictation from the spirit world, or—what I had in mind—spirit taking over your hand and doing the writing. Like with the black mirror, I haven't done enough practice to get the results I otherwise might.

We've had well over 150 participate. Several of the original group remain active and have become dear friends: Carol Brown, Chassie West, Sister Rosemarie Stevens, Kathleen Jenkins. Others come and go as they are able. Between twelve and twenty people join us from various parts of the world: the US, Canada, England, Hong Kong, Australia, and other areas. Regardless of where we live, though, when it comes to the spirit world, we all share similar experiences.

Over time, the group has branched into a variety of areas having to do with mediumship and spirituality. Sometimes, we chat about what we've been experiencing with Spirit, and sometimes we do a group meditation and attempt automatic writing, then share any messages that came through. Other times, we have guest speakers. It's all quite casual. Meetings are on the first and third Wednesday of each month at 5:30 p.m. pacific. Email me for an invitation: sheila@sheilalowe.com

I've written in earlier chapters about the Thomas fire, which destroyed around 1,000 homes in Ventura, where I live. It happened two months after the second symposium. I was far luckier than the six friends of mine who lost their homes, but that didn't stop me from freaking out.

I've always been intensely pyrophobic (I bet you're thinking, "you probably died in a fire in a past life," aren't you? I probably did.). Knowing that other people in California have had to drive right through fire to escape makes me feel like a total wimp, but looking out of my kitchen window and seeing the flames on the hillside about two miles away was beyond hair-raising.

A very strong Santa Ana wind was blowing, and moments after I looked out and saw the fire, the electricity went off. It was late at night and I was alone with Lexie the cat. I threw some things into a suitcase, put Lexie in her carrier, and drove across town. The traffic lights were out, the street signs swinging wildly in the wind.

My friend Marta met me at the Barnes & Noble parking lot. Her house was in another part of town in the danger zone. We sat up all night at her nearby business. Early the next morning, Marta went home and got there just in time to witness it burn to the ground.

What does this have to do with anything? After the Thomas fire, I tried and tried to meditate, but I no longer felt like I could make a connection. This was a repeat of what happened after I lost Jennifer.

I started meditating every day after her murder and was getting some good results. Six weeks after I buried my daughter, I hosted a conference that had been scheduled for a long time. People from all over the country had booked flights and hotels; I wasn't about to cancel the event. Then my first book was released and I went on a multi-state book tour, at the end of which, I attended an Afterlife conference out of state. At the end of that year of frenetic activity, near Jennifer's first anniversary, I was diagnosed with mononucleosis. I was down, and out for the count for more than a month.

Once I recovered from my illness, I could no longer meditate. So, when the same thing happened after the Thomas Fire, I started to wonder if maybe my subconscious connected meditating to bad things happening.

I don't have an answer, but I think it's a pretty good possibility.

Chapter 69
Mermaids galore

I resisted writing this book for more than twenty years. Mid-January, 2023, after receiving numerous messages through mediums that I needed to write something autobiographical, I finally started to think about it in earnest.

Lying in bed one night, I asked Jennifer to give me a sign that this was, indeed, what I was supposed to do, and if so, that she would help me with it. The sign should be something to do with mermaids, which I associate with her.

Note: rarely do I ask for signs, especially specific ones, although that's supposed to be the best way to do it. But this time, I did ask and I was specific. Not really expecting results, I put it out of my mind and drifted off to sleep.

The very next morning, I got a WhatsApp text from my daughter-in-law in Germany. Tuba sends me hundreds of photos and videos of my adorable little granddaughter, Cleo, for which I am immensely grateful. However, as rare as it is for me to ask for signs, it's virtually unheard of for her to text me.

Some Christmas gifts I had sent Cleo direct from Amazon had not arrived in time for the holiday, and I'd forgotten about them. On January 13, 2023 (which happens to be Arnie's birthday), here's what my daughter-in-law—the one who never texts me—wrote:

"...The dresses arrived yesterday and *a few days ago* the **mermaid** puzzle arrived as well..."

I had sent a set of doll clothes that included a mermaid costume. And, separately, some *Little Mermaid* puzzles (three and a half year-old Cleo is a fan). To get such a quick sign had me jumping up and down. The fact that the puzzle had already been there a few days, but it was on *this* day, after I'd asked Jen for a mermaid sign, that Tuba chose to tell me, was astonishing.

But that's not all. That night, I texted Ben about it. He texted back:

"Fifteen minutes ago, we were talking about a word for a particular use for Cleo. The word Cleo decided on was *Mermaid*."

But wait, there's more...

I was scheduled to make my third appearance at the Hillside Book Club four days after receiving my sign. The club had selected my latest "Beyond the Veil" book, *The Last Door*, and invited me to discuss it. The last time I had visited this group of awesome women was in October of 2017, when they read *What She Saw*, which became the prequel to the BtV series. WSS is the story of a young woman who wakes up on a train with amnesia. She debarks, unwittingly leaving a backpack, and any clues to her identity, behind.

That year, the book club met at the beautiful home of Irene, one of the members, on Halloween. The house stood high on a hill overlooking all of Ventura, as far the Pacific Ocean. Before the meeting started, I stood on the deck, admiring the twinkling lights of the city, fairylike in the darkness.

Irene was an incredible hostess and outdid herself with a meatloaf in the shape of a big, scary claw, Jello shots in syringes, and as many delectable Halloween-themed treats as you can dream up. There was also a great bonus surprise and thrill for me: the members all came dressed as characters from my book!

Amy Herron, de facto leader of the club, and her husband Jim, were FBI agents in dark suits, complete with badges. Teri, another member, came dressed as the backpack(!). She won a prize for Best Costume. Our host, Irene, wore the sparkly green dress of a mermaid.

(An aside: a short few weeks after the Halloween book club meeting, on December 4 (also the one-year anniversary of Arnie's transition to spirit), Irene's home was one of hundreds of casualties of the Thomas fire that swept through the entire Ondulando neighborhood).

So now, we're in 2023 at Amy's house. Apart from Amy and Dianne Maggio, who had both won character names in the book at one of my launch parties, I had seen very few of the club members in the five years since the Halloween meeting. As they began to arrive, Irene came over to greet me. After reintroducing herself she said, "I was the mermaid."

Another mermaid sign! I didn't say anything about it right away. First, we had a riotous Q&A and chat, then Amy played *Für Elise* on the piano—a composition that has meaning in *The Last Door*. As things were starting to wind down, I told the group how I had asked Jen for a mermaid sign, and that Irene had made a third reference. Amy then got excited and showed me her stemless wine glass, which her neighbor, Becky, had gifted to several friends. Painted on the glass were a mermaid and the words, "Mermazing Sisters."

I got the message. I was doing the right thing by starting this book, and Jen was going to help me with it.

The takeaway: ask for signs, and be specific.

$$\int$$

I've said that I don't often ask for signs, but here's one more from a while back when I asked Jennifer to let me know whether she was still around. That time, I wasn't specific, and when a couple of days passed with nothing happening, I figured either I was doing something wrong, or she wasn't listening, and forgot about it.

There was a dinner meeting I attended a couple of evenings later at the Ventura County Professional Women's Network. At the back of the room, a table is set up for members to show their wares. There were brochures about vitamins, a line of cosmetic products, and so on. I brought some of my books.

A newer member, Emily, had a display of hand-painted wooden signs. My friend and fellow author, James Gray, picked one that read "MEET THE

AUTHOR." Emily made miniature books and pasted on his covers. One of the several signs she had with her that Thursday night was a very pretty light green one that said in large letters, 'MERMAID CROSSING.'

Perfect, I thought as I handed over the $15. Jen loved mermaids; I'll buy it. It wasn't until I got home that it hit me: *Mermaid!* A wooden sign. I had asked for a sign and my daughter had sent me a *literal* sign. I could almost hear her laughing at her own joke.

And then it occurred to me: Mermaid CROSSING. Jen had crossed to the other side.

And then...

Not knowing how she felt about Spirit or the Afterlife, I was so excited about getting this sign that I shot off an email to Emily, the vendor. A short few minutes later, her reply landed in my inbox.

"You gave me chills," she wrote. She had been in her car in the driveway, preparing to leave for the meeting. Suddenly, she remembered a pair of earrings she had planned to show the VCPWN members. She hurried back to the house and put the earrings on.

Heading for the front door for the second time that evening, Emily got an urge to stop at her worktable. That was when she noticed the Mermaid Crossing sign and decided to take it with her to the meeting.

If that wasn't a *sign,* I don't know what is.

Chapter 70

Growing from the ashes

Almost from the moment I learned of her murder, I thought I would write my daughter's story. I even had a title: *Growing from the Ashes*. The trouble was, the story had such a sad ending, I couldn't bring myself to begin.

The years rolled by and I decided that writing articles and giving lectures about what had happened was enough; I didn't need to write an entire book.

My spirit guides had other ideas. After letting it go for seventeen years they began to hammer me with the same message:

Spirit says you need to write something different; something au-tobiographical. Jennifer will help.

Autobiographical? I didn't want to write a book about myself. Who would be interested enough to read it?

The messages continued coming via several independent mediums. Still resisting, I tried bargaining with Spirit. How about this, I suggested: as a published fiction author, I could write a paranormal story and share what I had learned about the Afterlife that way.

Expecting spirit to fully support the effort, I wrote *Proof of Life*, a story about a reluctant medium who had appeared in my earlier book, *What She Saw*. It's true that Jen gave me some help when I had questions, and so did

Arnie, who had crossed to spirit by then. But to my dismay, publishing the book did not put an end to the *"write something autobiographical"* messages.

Clearly, fiction wasn't going to cut it.

Finally, at the end of 2022, I decided I had better start listening. My dear friend Fiona had given me some notebooks for Christmas. I filled one of them with ideas of what I thought needed to be covered, and started writing the book on February 1st.

I'm not normally a fast writer—it usually takes me nine months to a year to finish a book. So, when the first draft was completed on February 25th, I was stunned. The only way that could have happened was to have Spirit, and Jennifer, working with me.

As I said in the previous chapter, the title was always *Growing from the Ashes.* You may have ideas about why, but there is a reason you may not have guessed.

⟨

Most people are familiar with the image of the mythical Phoenix—an immense immortal bird whose wingspan can reach as much as fifty feet. Legend has it that near the end of its life, which is at least five-hundred years, the Phoenix constructs a nest of fragrant boughs and spices on which it self-immolates—a funeral pyre from which it rises from the ashes, regenerating itself.

Scorpio, the astrological sign under which I was born, is considered the sign of death and rebirth, of letting go of attachments that no longer serve, and of transformation—stepping into a new form of being. Thus, the Phoenix is one of Scorpio's symbols.

Considering my fear of fire, it is perhaps ironic that I chose this image to represent my growth. But it is also appropriate. As my sign demands, I have burned it all down and started over, time and again—sometimes ignoring for too long the prodding of my spirit guides—but eventually getting it right.

Although I had already left the JW cult before the loss of my daughter in the physical world, it was that very loss that took me further on my path than any other experience. Like most parents, I would have done anything within my power to save her from that end. But an important truth I have come to understand is that everyone has their own journey. I could not walk Jennifer's path for her any more than she could have walked mine.

In the end, I am profoundly grateful that our oh-so-turbulent relationship has evolved into something beautiful and manifestly spiritual

Chapter 71

There is no death

I once prepared a handwriting analysis report for a personal client who loved what it said about her. But in her feedback, she made what struck me as an important point that I've never forgotten.

"This is really me!" she exclaimed. Then she hesitated. "But it's not *all* of me."

She was right, of course. There is no way a handwriting analysis or any other psychological test can possibly reveal 'all' of the writer—people are far too complex to be able to do that. Yet, their handwriting can reveal a great deal of important information about their core personality and the way the writer behaves and functions in their daily life.

In the same way, through the pages of this book, I've tried to share the core parts of who I am and why my journey has taken the sometimes-tortuous path that it has. But it is not possible—nor would I want—to reveal *everything* about myself. Everyone alive has millions of experiences that are pieces of our unique puzzles—our personal narrative. For me, one of the hardest parts of writing a memoir has been deciding what to include that might be interesting to others, and what to leave out that would be a dead bore to anyone but me. I hope I was successful.

Coming to the end of this story, I have one last thing to share.

Upon learning that I had finally undertaken this task, many of my friends have commented that they hoped it would be cathartic for me. The truth is, I have felt no need for catharsis, which is a process of releasing suppressed emotions and getting relief.

My chief aim in writing this memoir—or perhaps more accurately, autobiography (*I hear you, Spirit!*)—was to share my spiritual journey, which opened up upon my daughter's departure to the Other Side. Doing so required delving into my origins and showing why it took so long to open my eyes to what Spirit wanted me to see. And an important part of that process explains why Jennifer made some of the decisions she did that led, indirectly, to her murder.

My great desire is that the experiences I've chosen to share are ones that will help readers on their own path to better understanding life after earth. And, most of all, to learn, as I have learned, that there is no death. There is a wonderful life waiting to be lived after earth.

Blessings,

Sheila

Acknowledgments

I could make long lists of people who, over the years, have contributed to my growth, listened to me whine, and pushed me along my path, but someone would inevitably left out and feel bad. It gets to be like an Oscar acceptance speech. So, I'll just say "Thank you, you know who you are, I love you all, even if I haven't said so in this book."

My very close friend and colleague Linda Larson, for one. We have ridden the metaphorical waves together since 1984.

Writing a memoir has been a quite different experience from my other books, fiction and nonfiction, but there are still people to thank for their help and support.

And a very special thanks to Chassie West for her eagle copyediting eye and excellent feedback. Thanks, also to my beta readers, Nina Nelson, Pamela Asbury-Smith, Peg Brantley, Lauren Mooney Bear, and Marion Rollings. You all now know more of me than I ever intended to share. I think it's harder to be that open with people you know than those you don't!

Thanks, more than I can say, to Scott Montgomery for the stunning cover art and illustrations. I am so lucky and blessed that you took on this challenge.

Finally, thanks (I think) to my spirit guides and angels who insisted I complete this task. I hope I did it right.

Also By Sheila Lowe

FORENSIC HANDWRITING SERIES

POISON PEN

WRITTEN IN BLOOD

DEAD WRITE

LAST WRITES

INKSLINGERS BALL

OUTSIDE THE LINES

WRITTEN OFF

DEAD LETTERS

BEYOND THE VEIL SERIES

WHAT SHE SAW

PROOF OF LIFE

THE LAST DOOR

NONFICTION

READING BETWEEN THE LINES: Decoding Handwriting

ADVANCED STUDIES IN HANDWRITING

PSYCHOLOGY PERSONALITY & ANXIETY DISORDERS: How
They May Be Reflected in
Handwriting, and Other Important Topics

SUCCEEDING IN THE BUSINESS OF HANDWRITING ANALYSIS

IMPROVE YOUR LIFE WITH GRAPHOTHERAPY

THE COMPLETE IDIOT'S GUIDE TO HANDWRITING ANALYSIS

HANDWRITING OF THE FAMOUS & INFAMOUS

SHEILA LOWE'S HANDWRITING ANALYZER SOFTWARE

About the Author

Sheila Lowe is the author of eleven novels, including the award-winning Forensic Handwriting series and the Beyond the Veil paranormal suspense series. She is also a real-life forensic handwriting expert who testifies in court cases. In addition to writing stories of psychological suspense, she writes nonfiction books about handwriting and personality. She lives in Southern California.

To sign up for the newsletter: www.sheilalowebooks.com

Ways to reach Sheila

www.sheilalowebooks.com

https://www.sheilalowe.com

https://www.facebook.com/SheilaLoweBooks

https://www.instagram.com/sheilalowebooks/

https://www.goodreads.com/SheilaLowe

https://www.bookbub.com/authors/sheila-lowe

Dear Reader,

Did you enjoy *Growing From the Ashes?* If you did, please consider leaving a brief review on your favorite review site. It really helps when you tell others how you feel.

Get the latest on my books by signing up for updates at sheilalowebooks.com. I promise never to share your information.

Thank you so very much for spending this time with me. Be well,

Sheila

Printed in Great Britain
by Amazon

22370166R00143